ANGELA LORD is a designer, muralist an‹ Christchurch, New Ze‹ Gerard Wagner at the ‒‒‒‒‒‒‒‒ ‒‒‒‒‒‒ ‒‒‒‒‒‒‒‒ ‒‒‒‒‒‒ Painting School in Dornach, Switzerland. She teaches painting and offers a diploma recognised by the Art Section at the Goetheanum. Her publications include *The Archetypal Human-Animal, Rudolf Steiner's Watercolour Painting*; *The Archetypal Plant, Rudolf Steiner's Watercolour Painting*; *New Life – Mother and Child, The Mystery of the Goddess and the Divine Mother*; *Art, Aesthetics and Colour, Aristotle – Thomas Aquinas – Rudolf Steiner*; *Colour Dynamics*; *Easter, Rudolf Steiner's Watercolour Painting* and four books on Creative Form Drawing.

'The Human Being Finds Balance' by Gerard Wagner

LEMURIA

And our Fall from Paradise

Angela Lord

TEMPLE LODGE

Temple Lodge Publishing Ltd.
Hillside House, The Square
Forest Row, RH18 5ES

www.templelodge.com

Published by Temple Lodge 2024

A CIP catalogue record for this book is available from the British Library

ISBN 978 1 915776 22 8

Cover by Morgan Creative featuring 'Lemuria (after Rudolf Steiner)' by Angela Lord
Typeset by Symbiosys Technologies, Visakhapatnam, India
Printed and bound by 4Edge Ltd., Essex

Contents

'When one looks at the same things from many diverse aspects, the impressions one receives gradually complement each other to form an ever more animated picture. Only such pictures, not dry schematic concepts, can help the person who wants to penetrate into the higher worlds. The more animated and colourful the pictures, the more one can hope to approach the higher reality.'

– Rudolf Steiner, *Cosmic Memory*

Foreword

'And the Lord God planted a garden eastward in Eden; and there he put the human being whom he had formed. And out of the ground made the Lord God to grow every tree that is pleasant to the sight, and good for food; the tree of life also in the midst of the garden, and the tree of knowledge of good and evil.'

– Genesis 2: 8–9

Lemuria is a significant and fascinating phase of our past existence, holding many keys to our present and future stages of evolution. Through an understanding of its deeper aspects we can unlock its mysteries, and indeed some of the mysteries of world evolutionary processes.

Rudolf Steiner says:

> The primeval land mass of Lemuria lay between our present Australia and India. It was in the middle of the Lemuria phase that the higher triad of spirit-self (or manas), life-spirit (buddhi), and spirit-human (atma) united with the four lower principles of human nature: physical, etheric and the developing ego… Correctly speaking, the highest being on earth was not yet a physical human being in our sense of the word. Only a kind of sheath, or receptacle existed, made up of the highest animal-like nature, a being, or a collection, a group of beings, constituted of the four lower principles of human nature… which absorbed, as they individualised, the three higher principles which were contained in the heart of the Godhead… *As a result a drop of the independently individualised Divinity is to be found in each and every one of us, as human beings.**

_____

* Rudolf Steiner, *The Lord's Prayer*, Berlin, 28 January 1907.

The descent of manas, the spirit-self, during this middle-Lemurian phase was accompanied by the emotions of desire and passion. Before that time there had been no desire in the real sense as human beings were not warm-blooded. They had the same warmth as their environment, and in principle they could be likened to fishes.

This was expressed in the Bible, in Genesis, as: ' The earth was without form and void, and darkness was upon the face of the deep; and the Spirit of God was moving over the face of the waters.'

With the descent of the spirit-self, earthly desire and egotistic love entered humanity, and in the figure of Adam we recognise humanity of the Lemurian epoch, previously in soul-spirit realms, in its progress towards human existence in earthly corporeality.

> There is a significant connection between the name of the human being, Adam, and the term for earthly matter, 'adamah'. Adam is no individual name, neither does it mean 'man' in general. It specifically refers to 'one formed of earth substance'.*

The earthly domain, or kingdom, is the creation of the Godhead. Human beings at this stage were able to distinguish the great multiplicity of existence and life in this earthly realm as it emanated from the divine, and to name all its separate beings and features. 'Whatever the human being called every living creature, that was its name.' (Genesis 2:19.)

Rudolf Steiner observed that, 'if we could rise to penetrate what the names or conception or ideas of things really signify in spirit, we could see that it is the name that represents the wisdom which is in the divine sphere'.† For in our ancient past, wisdom and knowledge were bestowed upon us through the

---

* Emil Bock, *Genesis*, Chapter 1.
† Ibid.

wise guidance of mighty, protective and benevolent spiritual beings, the world creators, and their servers on earth, the initiates.

However, at times we are seemingly without constraint, rearranging the divine given order of things according to and suiting the perceptions of ourselves, the world and universe. But who is now directing and inspiring these perceptions and attitudes? Where and what are the sources of our complex materialistically-based world-views? And who or what are the driving forces behind our actions?

It is essential that we ask such questions and to search for honest answers. Crises and problems are lurking at the edges of our risky experiments with most of the sciences: technology, medicine, climate, botany, biology, gender, and with human consciousness itself.

This reflects our freedom. But are we pushing the boundaries too far?

By delving into our distant primeval past, we can discover the events which gradually brought about some remarkable changes in the course of world evolution and in our consciousness. Evolutionary processes continue today but are at present on a course of development towards what is becoming a troubled and fragile future.

We need to safeguard the ongoing development and fulfilment of the higher aspects of ourselves, which began to be united with the denser aspects of our constitution during Lemurian times.

This was symbolised in the mystery schools as follows:

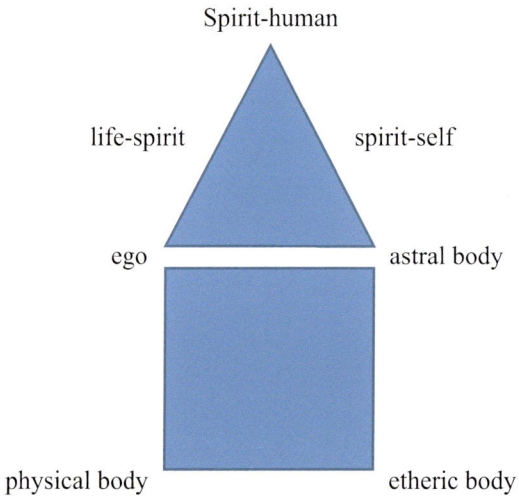

Spirit-human

life-spirit   spirit-self

ego   astral body

physical body   etheric body

Lemurian humanity chose and was granted freedom, but at a cost. It is now essential for our safe, stable and healthy future progress to choose and to create an environment and existence compatible with the higher disposition of our true being. Nothing less than the future of our world evolution is at stake.

PART ONE

Chapter 1
Earth's Evolution – An Overview of Early Geological Phases

'In the beginning God created heaven and earth.
And the earth was without form and void.'

— Genesis 1:1

Let's begin with an extended quotation from Hermann Poppelbaum:

> The evolution of the earth, as it is seen by supersensible perception, begins amid quite other conditions than those which natural science can describe. Everything that comes into being arises from a spiritual source... It is from the deeds of spiritual beings that evolution proceeds... The world of the spiritual, in which all events have their origin, is a world of active beings, filled with creative power, filled with the impulse to become... Just as the sense-world consists of things, so this original spirit-world consists only of beings... the highest in rank give the impulse; the next shape it, the lowest minister to it.
>
> Rank upon rank, reaching beyond one another and working into each other's hands, they cause the universe to come into being... The seed of the visible world arises out of the invisible... All the beings, present as the creators and witnesses of the earlier stages, take part in the later ones, but they have risen... to ever greater perfection. Others have remained behind: their activity will find its place later in a changed form. At each stage, like a new principle, something new is united with the earth's content.

... Not all the seed-organisms originally destined to become human could keep pace with evolution. At each stage, a number of them remained behind, to re-appear in the next stage as somewhat different forms... Thus there is laid the foundations of the three kingdoms below the human: animal, plant and mineral. Only the human kingdom has advanced uniformly, and at the earth stage has attained the body to be the bearer of an ego, an individuality. In the other kingdoms, the past lives on... but humans also carry in their structure traces of the past: the physical body we have in common with the minerals; the life-body with the plants, and the astral body with the animals, though all three are permeated with the ego, the true higher aspect of the human being... The gaps between the kingdoms of nature... are the persistent echoes of separate world epochs.*

The Geological Epochs

The beginning of the earth's mineralisation is marked by a recapitulation of the epochs of 'Old Saturn' (warmth ether); 'Old Sun' (light/air ether); 'Old Moon' (water ether) – but within the solidifying mineralisation of the earth. Rudolf Steiner stated that the periods named Azoic and Palaeozoic represent recapitulations of the far earlier Polarian and Hyperborean epochs. 'Just as the seed of the human being develops in the embryo period... and in doing so recapitulates in little form all the phases of humanity's development, so the earth at her birth into the mineral state recapitulates her own earlier spiritual stages.'†

Azoic Era (Archean or pre-Cambrian)

The earth is fluid, with gradual condensation of metals into liquids. With the appearance of the minerals, the earth's crust

---

* Hermann Poppelbaum, *Man and Animal*, Part II.
† Ehrenfried Pfeiffer, 1926.

gradually thickens and densifies into flowing lava, slowly becoming firmer. The plant and animal kingdoms resist solidification but exist as etheric archetypes, incorporating later into organisms which belong to the great order of invertebrates. They were already differentiated in their essential being, and their separation into types was an accomplished fact before the mineralisation of their bodily form set in. The ancestral forms existed in a bodily shape, but they were of a finer substantiality composed of air, warmth and water only. The seed-forms of the future human body were among those forms which resisted densification. Algae begins to appear.

Palæozoic Era (Cambrian, Ordovician, Silurian)

The plant and marine invertebrate kingdoms predominate. The coal and slate formations prevail with their essentially plant-like fossils. In the Cambrian period the animal groups (brachiopods and trilobites) take on a mineral body which shows that the hardening processes are intensifying. In the Silurian period the first primeval fishes and the first amphibians (to be found in coal deposits) are armoured like lower animals. An extraordinary range of animal forms comes to light. At this stage, the human being still retains a 'body' densified no further than the fluid condition. The human soul, or psyche, is still guided by higher spiritual beings and the human consciousness is plant-like or sleeping.*

Mesozoic Era (Carboniferous, Permian)

During this time the special qualities of the Lemurian epoch first come to full expression, distinguished by the incorporation of the solid element. The previous epochs were, in essence, still echoes of the Polarian and Hyperborean. Rudolf Steiner describes how this solidification was taking place too rapidly, creating inhospitable conditions on earth. At the beginning

---

* Paraphrased from Hermann Poppelbaum, op. cit.

of the Lemurian epoch, lower vertebrates (fishes and early amphibians) existed, and land plants diversified. Later, during the middle-Lemurian phase, cycads and ammonites appear; sharks develop, the coelacanth existed; amphibians were abundant and early reptiles appear. Towards the end of this middle phase (Permian), the reptiles surpass amphibians, trilobites become extinct, ferns and cyads are abundant.

Poppelbaum states: 'If we wish to form a picture of the structure of man's ancestor at the beginning of the Lemurian epoch we must think of the type of the lower vertebrates (fishes and amphibians) but in forms less densified than their descendants of the present day'.* The Permian and Triassic phases overlap the two great eras of the Palaeozoic and the Mesozoic, a span of 290–205 million years ago (according to natural science). The human being at this time had 'not yet taken up the solid element into himself'.†

---

* Paraphrased from *Man and Animal*, 'Mesozoic Era', op. cit.
† Ibid., 'Palæozoic Era'.

Chapter 2
Early Lemuria – Mud and Giant Oysters

'Nature being inconstant and taking pleasure in creating and making continually new lives and forms, because she knows that they augment her terrestrial substance, is more ready and swift in creating than time is in destroying… The animals serve as a type of the life of the world.'

– Leonardo da Vinci, from his notebooks

We find interesting descriptions of Lemuria in talks which Rudolf Steiner gave to workmen in 1922. These sessions arose from requests by workmen at the Goetheanum.* I quote excerpts from the talks, which were given on 20, 23 and 27 September of that year.†

> In an early stage of the earth's existence, when the moon and earth were still co-joined, the earth was of the consistency of a fairly thick sauce. In it floated living creatures that could be likened to giant oysters that were so enormous that you could have drawn all of France on their backs. The older ones of these animals were so huge because the earth as well was still huge.
>
> These creatures consisted of a jelly-like substance and wore a gigantic armour, like our turtles, and swam or moved around in the thickish liquid of the earth. They excreted slime, as do our present-day snails, which maintained the life of the earth, creating the earth as a whole into an egg. The moon within the earth bestowed upon those giant creatures the forces through which they could create these reproductive substances. The moon forces also

---

* This large building is situated in Dornach, near Basel in Switzerland. It is the world headquarters of the Anthroposophical Society.
† See Rudolf Steiner, *From Crystals to Crocodiles*.

exerted their influences, which resulted in a portion of these substances separating and floating off by itself in the liquid earth. When the sun shone upon this, an eggshell of sorts was formed. This caused the slime-like soft substance of the 'oyster' to expel the hard portion and thus a new creature came about. However, they left no fossil remains.

We can say that the female forces came from the moon, which was inside the earth, and the male, hardening forces, came from the sun which shone upon our soft globe from the outside. The secretions of the moon gave the earth the function of mother, while the sun produced the 'fatherly' substances in constantly creating those lumps of slime and surrounding them with a thick shell-like coating. They would not have been there if the sun had not been shining on them – they could not have existed without the sun.

The earth itself gave birth to these very clumsy, gigantic animals and was in turn fertilised by their secretion. The old ones died, but new ones developed out of the earth. We can imagine then that the earth was a living organism, a living being, sustained through the slime excreted by those creatures. The sun was shining upon this thick earth soup, and as a result certain areas within it thickened, which became the shells for the oysters. Underneath the thickened shell-mass, the slime was thinner, and these were kept alive by the moon within the earth... The moon is connected with all aspects of life. At the time of these giant oysters the moon was not separated from the earth, but dissolved in its thickish soup. It had no clear boundaries and just formed a sphere of slightly thicker material than the rest of the soft earth.

We could say that the earth had at one time its own reproductive energy, being fertilised by the sun and the huge oyster-like animals. And in turn, the moon forces within the earth were fertilised by the sun. It is interesting to note that even today oysters are considered to be an aphrodisiac… perhaps a tradition stemming from a memory of this ancient time? And how do oysters, as we know them now, produce pearls within them? We could wonder whether this process is a remnant of this ancient time, now condensed into a minute and exquisite form.

Walter Cloos writes:

> What is important for us in this picture is the idea of a life process that led to the formation of the armour-plated shells of these animals. This process was not localised anywhere in particular but extended over the whole earth and was part of the life of the earth.
>
> In Muschelkalk [Musselchalk] we have found a picture that represents a life process that we might call the 'oyster' stage of the earth. It was a preparatory stage for further differentiation of the animal world. The giant forms disappeared and the life of the earth as a whole dispersed itself into tiny forms which subsequently built up the mighty calcareous layers of the Jurassic and Chalk periods. At the same time there gradually arose the new giant forms of the saurians. This is the beginning of the new transition that leads to the mammal era… The life processes are connected with calcium carbonate… This is the form of calcium which is associated with the lower animals and the lower plants (algae). These lower organisms are the very first forms of life that have been preserved even in the very oldest strata.*

Rudolf Steiner adds:

> Back then there were no human beings as we know them… The surface of the earth consisted of a peculiar mud which contained various acids. Above the surface, the atmosphere

---

* Walter Cloos, *The Living Origin of Rocks and Minerals*, 'The Animal Nature and Limestone'.

contained all kinds of acids in gaseous form, even sulphuric and nitric acid gases, which were not very concentrated but in the air, in traces. This air was as warm as a warm oven. Above this layer was an even warmer one, which produced bolts of lightning and tremendous claps of thunder. At times the greenish-brown mud on the earth became as hard and compact as a horse's hoof, and then it dissolved again. Those times of hardening corresponded in a way to what we call winter. When the sun was shining in the summer, the mud liquefied again.

Human beings at this time existed in a vaporous cloud-like condition, organised and internally alive, but only dimly conscious. They moved and floated about, above the earth, surrounded and directed by higher beings, who could also enter into fully reciprocal relationships with them. Dreaming, instinctive, almost unconsciously-striving humanity existed in an upwardly-orientated longing towards understanding, while the beings in their surroundings were filled with wisdom and directed themselves downwards towards the earth, still in its mud-oyster phase.*

This stage of development refers to the human condition as a 'fire-cloud', which, in its cloudy floating existence contrasts considerably with the huge oyster-like beings described above.

---

* Rudolf Steiner, *Cosmic Memory*, 'Extrusion of the Moon'.

Chapter 3
Fish-Lizards and Fire-Birds

'And God said, Let the waters bring forth abundantly the moving
creatures that have life, and fowl that may fly above the earth in
the open firmament of heaven. And God created great whales,
and every living creature that moves, which the waters brought
forth abundantly, after their kind, and every winged fowl after
his kind: and God saw that it was good. And God blessed them,
saying, Be fruitful and multiply, and fill the waters in the seas,
and let fowl multiply on the earth.'

– Genesis 1: 20-22

The earlier Earth-condition later developed into a different one during which peculiar animals lived in the air. Their tails were flat and covered with scales; their wings and heads resembled those of bats. They were able to emit something like electricity and to send it down to the earth. They were small dragon-birds and had extraordinarily keen senses. Eagles and vultures which developed out of these ancient birds after many metamorphoses, retained only the keen sight of their ancestors. Their wings were particularly sensitive, and when the moon was shining they flapped their wings simply because they experienced such a pleasant sensation in them. They enjoyed the moonlight, and could create delicate clouds of fire around them, which only fireflies can do nowadays. When the moon shone, these dragon-birds shone and shimmered and glowed like fireflies. They also responded to starlight, which gave a pleasing sensation in their wings, with the result that their wings became speckled. Imprints of fossils which are found in limestone show, on close examination, traces of all sorts of stars on the fossilised wing imprints. These are traces of the stars' impressions. When the sun shone they absorbed substances from the air, which they sucked in as nourishment, and digested them in the warm sunshine. (We could wonder whether the feathers on the breast of a speckled thrush, or speckled bird's eggs, are a long-distant remnant of this.)

On the earth below, however, lived gigantic animals, half swimming and half wading in the mud – the ichthyosaurs, literally 'fish-lizards'. Their head was like a dolphin's and their body like that of a huge lizard covered with thick scales. They had huge triangular teeth like a crocodile, and soft fins which helped them move, half swimming, half wading, through the mud. But the strangest thing about these creatures was that they had huge eyes which emitted light. If you had been alive, then you would have seen 'electrical' dots up in the clouds, especially during moonlit nights when the shining birds liked to fly around, and at dawn you would have seen gigantic lights coming towards you with a body larger than a whale and fins to swim through the soft mud.

Further down in the mud lived other animals who thoroughly enjoyed wading and wallowing in the mud and always looked very dirty, covered with greenish-brown mud. These were the plesiosaurs, who had whale-like bodies, covered with scales. They often settled themselves comfortably on the firmer mud, and then swam like huge boats through the mud-soup. They had four legs, which although ungainly with hand-like feet, helped them to walk on the firmer mud.

This is the way things were on the ancient earth. The plesiosaurs led a lazy life down in the mud, and the ichthyosaurs swam and also flew around just above the ground. Above them hovered the shining clouds of the dragon-birds who were attracted by the shining eyes of the ichthyosaurs, allowing themselves to fall into their jaws and be eaten. The dragon-birds blissfully threw themselves into the huge jaws, but the ichthyosaurs felt uncomfortable in their stomachs because electricity developed there. These huge creatures gradually became weaker, suffering more and more from stomach aches! They, and the plesiosaurs who also ate a few dragon-birds, gradually changed themselves and slowly, over time, developed into different animals, metamorphosing their bodies. They also needed to adjust to different conditions on the earth, which began to rotate slightly more quickly, causing substances to precipitate out of the air and to unite with the earth.

The air became foggy, and the muddy earth became more compact. Huge fern-like plants grew in the foggy air, sinking roots into the thickening muddy earth. Thousands and thousands of years later, different animals lived in the mud, with huge stomachs, heads like plump seals, darkened eyes, four clumsy feet and bodies covered with fine hair. These were plant-eaters, moving around in the gigantic forests, eating as much as they could with their huge jaws. These animals have descendants in the sea-cows.

The dragon-birds also, over thousands of years changed their shape, because the air no longer contained the same substances as before. They gradually moved down, closer to the earth, and later became birds. On the earth, animals were always being transformed through what they ate, and all that is left of these ancient creatures, although now in much smaller form, are turtles and crocodiles.*

* Paraphrased from Rudolf Steiner, *From Crystals to Crocodiles*, 20, 23 & 27 September 1922.

'Lemuria (after Rudolf Steiner)' by the author

PART TWO

Chapter 4
Warmth, Light, and the Music of the Spheres

'Something in us sings an ascendant song, and we expect we know not what: something in us sings a decrescent song, and we realise vaguely the stirring of immemorial memories.'

— Fiona Macleod, 'Fragments'

Rudolf Steiner spoke of the time before the sun departed from the earth:

> Think of a new-born child which still has a quite soft place on top of the head. Imagine this place quite open and imagine a warmth-current coming from outside into this opening... and these streaming warmth-forces go down to form a kind of centre where the heart is.*

He went on to say that originally the human being actually consisted of flowing currents of warmth, and later in evolutionary processes the human heart, with its blood vessels and structures, arose out of this rudimentary warmth-current. Our whole human form began from the heart, formed from warmth.

Streaming forces of warmth also projected outwards from humans when they were still horizontal beings, swimming about in the water-ether. This was an etheric lantern-like 'organ', protruding from the upper area of the head, and it sensed the water temperature, indicating colder and warmer areas, guiding the directions to swim to. As such, it was not

---

* Rudolf Steiner, *The Influence of Spiritual Beings upon Man*, Berlin, 16 March 1908.

really an eye. 'So we have something like a goblet-shaped organ spreading downwards to the first rudiments of the heart, and surrounded by something like prehensile arms, while up above one would have a sort of warmth-sensing organ.'* Warmth-matter gradually condensed to air, allowing light to enter, shining inwardly, and the warmth-organ of the human-being began to radiate light, like a lantern.

With the surrounding air, human beings began to develop the beginnings of a breathing process; and the streams of light developed the beginnings of an inner nerve-system.

After the separation of the sun, there existed one cosmic body of the earth and moon joined together. The former gaseous condition condensed to water, and substances densified. Forces of illumination had departed with the sun, and there was darkness again on the earth. 'However, human beings' earliest nerve-system had the power to create inner light-pictures, or colour-filled visions. Clairvoyant consciousness arose... the powerful gift of clairvoyance.'†

On the earth, as the water condensed, it was vibrated through and through by sound, and currents of tone created forms in the water:

> The instreaming music from cosmic space gave rise to most manifold forms and figures, and the substances dissolved in the water, which were themselves watery, listened to the cosmic music and arranged themselves in conformity to it... The original albumen was formed of cosmic substance that had been formed by the harmonies of world-cosmic tone.‡

The water, congealed to albumen, moved along the streaming lines of warmth, and gradually became, in the course of time, what would become blood. The congealed water established

---

* Ibid.
† Ibid.
‡ Ibid.

itself as albumen in the nerve-lines, and also formed a kind of covering, a cartilaginous gluten, as a protective outer layer. All of these movements and transformations took place through the cosmic influences of the music of the spheres.

The heart proceeded from the warmth-element; the breathing system born of the air, the nerve-system born of the light. Then came the protoplasmic material which inserted itself into the organs and formed the whole to living matter through the cosmic tones congealing the fluid substances… The glandular system arose out of this living material… Shortly before the departure of the moon a condition of earthly solidness came about and the processes of mineralisation began.*

External mineral combustion created a substance within the earth-mass, which is described in occultism as 'ash'. The ash embedded itself in the structure of the combined earth and moon… In human beings ash substances, made up of many varied minerals, were taken in and absorbed… How did the ash press into the albuminous substance? … It was the sense of the word, the first dawning in human consciousness which later became internalised as thought… The actual mission of earthly evolution, that in which Love comes to expression in the human being, was laid down first within our warmth… then Spirit was there in the form of air and light; then came the incorporation of the organic through the wonder-working of world music. Only then was the whole impregnated with mineral substance, solid matter, through the word, or thought.†

The last developed part of human beings were the sense-organs, which had not yet opened at this stage. Then the moon, with its coarse hardening beings and processes, left the earth,

---

* Ibid.
† Ibid.

allowing the developing human beings to move into a higher condition. The two heavenly bodies of sun and moon were now outside, sustaining a mutual balance. They opened the human senses.

Only relatively later, as a final formation, the cell developed. 'Organisms have never formed themselves out of cells, but the cell has formed itself out of the living.'*

---

* Ibid.

Chapter 5
Our Planetary Sojourn

'While we are asleep, our ego and our astral body return to the spiritual world, to the world of our origin which we left in order to become earth people... Every night we are divided among our counterpart of the universe of stars and the planets.'

– Rudolf Steiner, Oslo, 18 May 1923*

Before the separation of the moon, the moon forces brought about an increasing solidification in the earth. Some humans found it more difficult to incarnate, to return to the earth from the spiritual worlds due to the increasing hardening processes, which were exerting too strong an influence on their physical bodies. Rudolf Steiner wrote that:

> ...their form was much too hardened, and under the influence of the moon forces had grown too unlike the human figure to be able to receive the soul. This meant that certain human souls no longer found it possible to return to earth... Only the most mature, only the strongest felt themselves equal to the task of so transforming the earthly body during its growth that it could blossom into the true human form. Hence only some of the human bodily descendants became vehicles for earthly human beings. Others, owing to their hardened form, could only receive souls that were at a lower level than the souls of human beings... these eventually became the ancestors of the animal kingdom. In the course of time they evolved organs which existed only as appendages in human beings, and they had souls which could not dwell in only one single creature.†

---

* Rudolf Steiner, *Life Beyond Death*, 'Our Experiences during the Night and the Life after Death'.
† Rudolf Steiner, *Occult Science, An Outline*.

The group-souls of the animals developed, whereby one soul lived in a number of animal forms which were related and almost identical in appearance. In our times we speak of a herd of cows, a flock of sheep, a pack of wolves, or a herd of elephants. This grouping together of many animals, almost identical in appearance and often reacting as one, is the outer embodiment of a group soul, which guides the physical animals with great wisdom. When an animal, fish, bird or insect dies, it re-joins its group soul in the spiritual worlds.

And what of the human beings who, although advancing further, nevertheless found the earth conditions more and more unsuitable? Where did they go? How did they continue their existence? Because they could no longer live on earth, their development continued in other places, in other heavenly regions, which we can refer to as the 'planetary spheres'.

Some went to the planet whose physical expression is known as Jupiter, which under the guidance of cosmic beings had already received human beings into its own realm, at an earlier stage, in order to continue their evolution. And at a still earlier phase, when the earth-moon and the sun were united and air was being incorporated, some human beings even then were affected too strongly, and withdrew to the spiritual realm of Saturn. Others, during the Lemurian time of densification, found in the Mars sphere a place suited to their further evolution.*

Were it not for the separation of the moon from out of the earth, all human souls may have had to leave the earth, so inhospitable and uninhabitable had it become that only a few humans could remain. We must remember, however, that

_____

* Detailed descriptions can be found in Rudolf Steiner's *Occult Science, An Outline* and *Cosmic Memory*, Chapters 6 and 7.

the human 'body' was soft and pliable, existing mainly in the earth's circumference, only gradually descending over the course of thousands of years, guided by beings of love and beings of wisdom.

> I am as Soul
> Not only on the Earth
> But in water, air and fire.
> In my Fire-being
> I am in the Planets and the Sun;
> In my Sun-being
> I am in the heaven of the fixed-stars.

> I am as Soul
> Not only on the Earth
> But in light, word and life.
> In my Life-being
> I am within the planetary-and-Sun-being,
> In the Spirit of Wisdom;
> In my Wisdom-being
> I am in the Spirit of Love.

'Adam Kadmon in Early Lemuria' by Rudolf Steiner.
Pastel sketch

PART THREE

Chapter 6
Self-Impregnation and Clairvoyance

'When from depths of soul
The spirit turns to cosmic existence
And beauty wells from wide expanses,
Then out of heavens' distances
Strength of life streams into human bodies
Uniting by its mighty power
Spirit being with human existence.'
– Rudolf Steiner, *Calendar of the Soul* (Verse 52)

In an early phase of Lemurian existence, human beings were soft and malleable, carrying the nature of man and woman within themselves to a balanced, equal degree. The soul-life gave expression, gave form, to a body which embraced male and female at the same time, for the soul is simultaneously both male and female. It carries these two natures within itself – its male element, or aspect, related to will, and its female element to imagination.

At that time, the human soul was able to pour its whole being into its form, into its 'outer' mobile, soft physicality. Being and gesture were as one, a unified expression or manifestation of inner and outer in harmony with itself.

Every human being could create, or produce, another human being out of itself. When a new human being separated from their parent identity, they appeared as a truly articulated organism, but incomplete. Further development of their organs occurred outside the parental entity, brought about through a force similar to our present-day will-power. In order that this development took place, that the new human being could mature, the parent needed to care for its offspring. This it did by focusing its own power as an activity of gathering and contracting external warmth and confining it to a certain space, surrounding the young organism with the warmth it needed for its maturation. Some organs were cast off; others, which were quite incomplete to begin with, were later developed more fully.

The most highly organised and developed organs were those of motion, followed by hearing and perception of hot and cold – an early sense of touch which was related to the surroundings. The soft, flexible body was warm-blooded, and was able to sense, to feel the surrounding environment within its own inner structures. This outer environment was intimately and directly experienced by the soul, and every single disturbance affected it, especially through the sense of hearing. In turn, the soul's own activities were an echo, a response, to these impressions. The soul transformed its perceptions of sound coming from the surroundings into activity, into actions.

When their actions could proceed without any hindrances, human beings experienced pleasure, but when they were hindered in any way, they felt displeasure and even discomfort. It was the absence or presence of hindrances to their will that determined the content of human beings' inner sensations of joy and pain. When they could be completely free in their actions, beautiful transparent, light images lived in human souls, but when they experienced obstacles or hindrances, then dark, misshapen images arose within them.

In a way, the soul-life of the average early Lemurian was relatively instinctive and dreamlike, with many of their activities being influenced by the course of the sun and moon: when they were active or resting; how they regulated their food intake, and how they could only self-impregnate at certain times. Coloured-images related to their inner life and its responses to their external activities and experiences filled their consciousness. This was not a mirroring, but colourful, independent inner images arose within them. This is what could be termed as an instinctive, imaginative clairvoyance.*

---

* Rudolf Steiner, *Cosmic Memory*, 'The Last Periods Before the Division into the Sexes'.

Chapter 7
Reproduction – Adam and Eve

'So God created the human being in His own image…
Male-and-female He created them. And God blessed them and
said to them, "Be fruitful and multiply."'

— Genesis 1: 27-28

The middle Lemurian phase saw processes of reproduction taking place in several ways: sweat-born, egg-born and androgyny. According to *The Secret Doctrine*,*

> … almost sexless in its early beginnings, it became bisexual or androgynous, very gradually of course. This transformation required numberless generations, during which the simple cell that issued from the earliest parent (the two in one), first developed into a bisexual being: and then the cell, becoming a regular egg, gave forth a unisexual creature. In the Third Race, humankind is the most mysterious… it is evident that the units of this race began to separate in their pre-natal shells or eggs, and to issue out of them as distinct male and female offspring, ages after the appearance of its early progenitors… Toward the end of the Fourth sub-race the babe gained its faculty of walking as soon as liberated from its shell, and by the end of the Fifth, humankind was born by the same processes as our historical generations. This of course, required millions of years.

From her clairvoyant observations, Blavatsky also concluded that it was only after the separation of the sexes, when their bodies had become increasingly dense and physical, that these entities became more human, even in appearance.

---

* H.P. Blavatsky, *The Secret Doctrine*, Vol. II.

There are further interesting observations made by Blavatsky, which read in an almost biblical way:

> During the Third Race the boneless animals grew and changed, they became animals with bones, their chayas (bodies) became solid. The animals separated first. They began to breed. The two-fold human beings separated also. He said, 'Let us as they; let us unite and make creatures'. They did.
>
> And those that had no spark took huge she-animals unto them. They begat upon them dumb races. Dumb they were themselves, but their tongues untied. The tongues of their progeny remained still. Monsters they bred. A race of crooked red-hair-covered monsters going on all fours. A dumb race to keep the shame untold.

Another ancient commentary adds:

> …when the Third race separated and fell into sin by breeding human-animals, these animals became ferocious, and humans and they, mutually destructive. Until then there was no sin, no life taken. Seeing which the Lhas wept, saying 'The Amanasa [the mindless] have defiled our future abode. This is Karma. Let us dwell in the others. Let us teach them better lest worst should happen.' They did. Then all human beings became endowed with manas. They saw the sin of the mindless.

We can gather from *The Secret Doctrine* that Blavatsky considered that these semi-humans dwindled in size, and gradually, over centuries, became more densely physical, culminating in a race of apes during the Miocene period.

Although these observations differ from those of Rudolf Steiner's, both in their descriptive and interpretive aspects, it is interesting to consider this cradle of earliest humanity from different aspects, for by doing so we gain a multifaceted overview of our early existence, and begin to realise how extraordinary our journey has been – and still can be.

Rudolf Steiner observed, from the Akashic Records, that the division into male and female took place as the earth became more dense, and the human bodies also. Early Lemurian times saw the human being as being dreamlike, quite dull in consciousness. The forces (or energy) for reproduction required organs in the human constitution which could create new offspring through a single-sexed process of re-creation, in other words, to an equal degree the nature of man and woman were carried within themselves:

We must picture to ourselves that in the times preceding dual sexuality, fertility took place in quite a different way. Clairvoyant vision can see that fertility happened with the intake of food, and those beings which in those early times were male–female received fertilising forces with their food. This food was, of course, still of a much more delicate nature, and when human beings partook of nourishment in those times, there was something else contained in these nourishing fluids which gave these beings the possibility of producing another being of like kind.

The nourishing foods imbibed from the surroundings by these beings of a dual sexual nature had the power of fertilisation only at quite definite times. This depended on the changes that took place which are comparable to today's seasonal changes...

The beings that were still undivided into two sexes were outwardly very similar, and their characters were more or less the same too. A great uniformity was there then... When the human being was still more etheric and not so firmly embedded in matter, then at birth and for some time afterwards... they were in a certain way all fundamentally alike. However, they did not remain the same all their lives because influences coming into them from their surrounding environment brought about tremendous changes in them.*

Their bodies were soft and malleable and the earth more fluid. Initially, the human soul could influence substances in order to re-create from itself, but as this activity changed with processes of densification, the human soul gained the capacity for thinking. A dreaming soul-life began to awaken as the bodily constitution changed. As new organs of reproduction were being formed, so developed a transformation in consciousness: humans awoke as new organs developed, namely an elementary formation of what would later become our brain. We would now be able to connect sense-perceptions with thought.

The division into two sexes took place as the moon departed from the increasingly hardening earth. This brought about the possibility of greater individualisation through the male element. The interaction of male and female resulted in spiritual godliness being gradually lost, when human beings were seeing the surrounding sense-world more and more clearly. They were no longer in full harmony with the divine-spirited cosmos but began to follow their own impulses. To begin with, however, sexual love in all its aspects was noble and pure, and regarded as being sacred. It was, in part, still directed by higher individualities and was not yet sensual but quite dreamlike.

This transformation took place slowly and gradually, the metamorphosis of one-sided physical fertilisation becoming twofold, giving a new possibility for creative faculties of soul and spirit to develop. Rudolf Steiner wrote:

>...both the male soul in the female body and the female soul in the male body again become double-sexed through

---

* Rudolf Steiner, *The Being of Man and His Future Evolution*, Berlin. 8 December 1908.

fructification by the spirit. Thus man and woman are different in their external form; internally their spiritual one-sidedness is rounded out to a harmonious whole. Internally spirit and soul are fused into one unit. Upon the male soul in woman the action of the spirit is female, and thus renders it male-female; upon the female soul in man the action of the spirit is male, and thus renders it male-female also. The double-sexedness of the human being has retired from the external world, where it existed in the pre and early Lemurian time, into the human interior.

One can see that the higher essence of a human being has nothing to do with man or woman. The inner equality, however, does result from a male soul in woman and correspondingly from a female soul in man. The union with the spirit finally brings about the equality.*

In our earthly evolution, then, we have taken a journey through the senses. Our earlier automatic dreamlike experiences of the spiritual worlds – which were direct, acquired through a natural clairvoyance and connected to our unconscious, or innocent, capacity to reproduce – have now become a challenge for our inner, modern thinking consciousness: that of inwardly re-creating our knowledge and experiences of the spirit through our own individual striving.

The gradual descent into the sensory world is termed 'the Fall', as in the biblical term. We now have our freedom to work on processes within our inner soul-life which can lead to a rebirth, in a spiritual sense, in the future. We chose to fall in order to gain this freedom

---

* Rudolf Steiner, *Cosmic Memory*, 'The Division into the Sexes'.

Chapter 8
The Mystery of the Fall and the Development of Love

'The soul's creative might
Strives outward from the heart's own core
To kindle and inflame god-given powers
In human life to right activity;
The soul thus shapes itself
In human loving and in human working.'
– Rudolf Steiner, *Calendar of the Soul* (Verse 41)

There are many questions we can ask about the Garden of Eden and the seemingly tragic expulsion from it. Why was this necessary? Why were the consequences so severe? How does this play into our present circumstances, our future?

Recalling that the descent into earthly matter was a gradual process, taking place over many thousands of years, we can begin to understand the deeper processes active in world and human evolution. Yes, we reap the consequences: food requires intensive labour to produce, and work in order to purchase it; women suffer pain during childbirth; and we are no longer consciously aware of our connection to the creative divine gods who are sustaining us and our world.

We have been granted a perilous freedom, which has given rise to all the complex problems we have created for ourselves and for our world. What lies behind all this? How have we ended up in this condition? And, where is it leading to? Powerful forces are at work within the human soul for good and evil, and our souls are a battleground between the forces of hatred and destruction and the powers of compassion.

Putting it simply, we have the capacity to destroy ourselves and our earthly home, or to co-create with active forces of goodness. We are free to choose, and we always have a choice because we have been granted the gift of free will. This is the mystery of the Fall.

Rudolf Steiner observed that,

...if we were to see the original human bodies of the Lemurian Age, we should find that they represented the extreme limit of ugliness, and human beings become more and more ennobled as love increasingly purified them. And humanity will evolve even beyond our present human form. In the future our external physiognomy will show what qualities lie within our soul.*

He describes that our inner life will no longer be concealed within us, but will, in the distant future, be visible in our outer appearance. Goodness and nobility will shape our physiognomy as well as debasement and evil. Our inner soul-spiritual striving will shape our countenance and gradually our bodily nature will become increasingly refined and spiritualised. This will be in contrast to those remaining enmeshed in materialism and evil, whose bodies will become hardened and distorted.

Our present world, with all its manifest beauty lying within the mineral, plant and animal kingdoms, has been created, permeated and imbued with wisdom – filled with wisdom from spiritual beings during the Ancient Moon phase of evolution. The Moon phase could be termed 'the Cosmos of Wisdom', and the Earth phase, 'the Cosmos of Love'.

In order that love might develop on earth, love had to be inaugurated in the initial phase (in Lemuria) as sex-love, in order to rise through the various stages and finally, when the perfected earth has reached its last phases, will be developed in humanity as pure spiritual love. Earthly

---

* Rudolf Steiner, *The Influence of Spiritual Beings Upon Man*, Berlin, 24 March 1908.

humanity is to develop love so that it may be given back to the earth, for all that is developed in the microcosm is, in the end, poured out into the macrocosm. The wisdom of the past Moon-phase shines towards the earthly-humans as the wisdom which permeates their structure.

The love which is developed by humanity during this Earth epoch will permeate the future Jupiter phase of evolution with a sweet perfume. Love will stream forth to them in fragrance. Just as wisdom shines towards us on the earth, so in the future will there come fragrantly towards the exalted spiritual beings of the Jupiter phase, that which is now evolving here on earth as love… Thus will the grades of love stream out as perfume ascending the cosmos… Human beings living on earth today are the instruments of the evolution of love.*

This is indeed the true aim of our existence. It lies encompassed within our world religions, our moral integrity, humility, compassion, tolerance, truthfulness, our search for knowledge and understanding, and our striving for freedom.

Teacher, which is the greatest commandment in the law? And Jesus said to him 'You shall love the Lord your God with all your heart and with all your soul and with all your mind… And you shall love your neighbour as yourself. On these two commandments depend all the law and the prophets.†

_____

* Ibid. (Paraphrased.)
† *The Gospel of Matthew*, 22: 36-40.

'Jehovah and the Luciferic Temptation – Paradise' by
Rudolf Steiner. Pastel sketch

'Adam and Eve (The Tree of Knowledge)' by Gerard Wagner

PART FOUR

Chapter 9
The Human Kingdom

'… in evolution, considered from the physical aspect, there arises the distinction between bodies which are more capable of per-fection and which still remain flexible, and those which become less capable of perfection and gradually harden… This difference becomes particularly critical shortly before the separation of the moon in the Lemurian epoch.'

– H. Poppelbaum, *Man and Animal*

The following descriptions are paraphrased from W. Scott-Elliot's *The Story of Atlantis and the Lost Lemuria*. They pro-vide fascinating details, many very similar to those of Rudolf Steiner's, while others differ, giving us a wider perspective.

The early Lemurian human being, 'must be regarded rather as an animal destined to reach humanity … but had not yet received the divine spark which should endow them with mind and individuality … Their bodies would have appeared to us as gigantic phantoms, indeed if we could have seen them at all, for their bodies were formed of astral matter.'

The following phase developed an etheric body, and in a third phase, 'their bodies had become material, being com-posed of gases, liquids and solids … but the gases and liquids predominated, for as yet their vertebrate structure had not solidified into bones such as ours, and they could, therefore, not stand erect…'

'The organs of vision of these creatures were of a rudi-mentary nature, at least such was the condition of the two eyes in front with which they sought for their food upon the ground. But there was a third eye at the back of the head, the pineal gland, which was the chief centre of astral and physical sight.'

Slowly the gigantic, gelatinous body began to solidify, and the soft-boned limbs developed into a bony structure, somewhat before the middle of the Lemurian period. These 'primitive creatures' could now stand upright, being able to walk backwards with as much ease as forwards.

The following is a description of a man who belonged to one of the later so-called 'sub-races' (which, it should be noted, have nothing to do with the races on earth today):

His stature was gigantic, somewhere between 12 and 15 feet. His skin was a yellowish-brown colour. He had a long lower jaw, a strangely flattened face, eyes small but piercing and set curiously far apart, so that he could see sideways as well as in front, while the eye at the back of the head – on which part of the head no hair grew – enabled him to see in that direction also. He had no forehead, and the head sloped upwards and backwards in a rather curious way. The arms and legs were longer in proportion than ours (especially the arms) and could not be perfectly straightened at the elbows or knees. The hands and feet were enormous, and the heels projected backwards in an ungainly way. The figure was draped in a loose robe of skin, something like a rhinoceros hide, but more scaly. Round his head, on which the hair was quite short, was twisted another piece of skin to which were attached tassels of bright red, blue and other colours. In his left hand he held a sharpened staff, about the height of his own body, about 12 or 15 feet. In his right hand was twisted the end of a long rope made of some creeping plant, by which he led a huge and hideous reptile, somewhat resembling a plesiosaurus. The Lemurians actually domesticated these creatures and trained them to hunt other animals.

Many were less human in appearance than the individual described above. Further developments came about later.

> While retaining the projecting lower jaw, the thick heavy lips, the flattened face, and the uncanny looking eyes, they had by this time developed a forehead, while the curious projection of the heel had been considerably reduced. In one branch of this 7th sub-race, the head might be described as almost egg-shaped – the small end of the egg being uppermost, with the eyes wide apart and very near the top. He was considerably shorter than the earlier man described before… These people developed an important and long-lasting civilisation, and for thousands of years dominated most of the tribes who dwelt on the vast Lemurian continent, and towards the end they secured another long lease of life and power by inter-marriage with the Rmoahals – the first sub-race of the Atlanteans.

This was not simply 'the survival of the fittest' but a long, complex interweaving of groups, tribes and indeed whole 'races' of early humanity whose aptitudes, qualities and capacities were being gradually developed and protected in order to further world evolution. The progress of humanity was a complicated and intricate process, which at times saw regression, degeneration and a dying out of certain groups, and a forward-surging civilising advancement of others. The more highly developed leaders and guides directed migrations to ensure humanity's furtherment, bringing about cross-breeding between the most advanced Lemurians with the earliest peoples of the completely new phase of the Atlantean period.

Chapter 10
Becoming Upright : Balancing, Moving, Walking

'To understand the human being we must reach into all the mysteries involved in the being of nature as well as in the spirit of the cosmos. Ultimately, human beings are intimately connected with all the mysteries of nature and with universal spirituality.'

— Rudolf Steiner, 18 November 1923

There are truly remarkable processes taking place in early childhood as children learn to stand upright, to balance, move and walk. We can be amazed at the young child's perseverance and excitement as their first few wobbly steps gradually become more stable and certain.

In a way, this activity can be understood as a recapitulation of the earliest phases which humanity undertook in Lemuria. We could regard the whole of humanity as a being in its infancy at this time, gradually learning to stand upright from its primal condition of being horizontal. Anthroposophical understanding of embryology and early childhood can reveal the earliest stages of earthly development, as many thousands of years of evolution are encapsulated within the concentrated time span of 18-24 months of pregnancy, birth, babyhood and early childhood.

Travelling back in time sees Lemuria as a seething, volatile turmoil of activity – fiery and explosive. (The typical two-year-old, you might mutter!) Human beings were initially not upright; we had to become so. How was this accomplished? Rudolf Steiner provides us with an astonishing insight:

> Our planet earth is partly built up through the melting and glowing of metals in the forces of fire. As we look back to

ancient times when planet earth was being built, we see in the metal, melting through the heat of fire, an aspect of the works of the seraphim, cherubim and thrones in the earthly world. We can look back… and see how metals glowed and liquefied as they were melting in fire… The thrones had an especially active role in this, with the seraphim and cherubim quietly working alongside.

It is the cherubim, however, who play the main role when children learn to walk, talk and think… We observe in children how their whole orientation in life begins with attaining an upright posture; we witness the activity of the marvellous forces whereby children find their way dramatically into the world… If we observe how we actually build and shape ourselves in the world of the senses, we see formative forces quietly at work.

When we observe a child learning to walk and talk and think, we see in their actions a mimicking, a copying of the older children and adults around them. But there is another, hidden aspect to this wonderful process: We can consider the spiritual processes which actually enabled them to learn to walk and speak. The archetype of this capacity, this power, is revealed if we witness the melting of metals when exposed to fire, when flames take hold of the metal, making it flow. As metal becomes fluid, it becomes more volatile, and we can have a clairvoyant perception of the inner resemblance between that process, and the smelting and volatilising process in cosmic fires that enable a little child to walk, to speak and to think. And we realise that the beings of the first hierarchy, the seraphim, cherubim and thrones are involved in this two-fold activity.

… Such knowledge reveals a kinship between the cosmic fires by which metals are melted and the powers that make us truly human.*

_____

* *At Home in the Universe*, 'Earth and the Mystery of Karma', 18 November 1923.

From this extraordinary observation, we can then imagine that there is a connection between the fiery conditions of early Lemuria and the processes which primal humanity underwent in order to achieve uprightness, to balance and to move about vertically.

> As the metals melted, majestic flames of the fires' forces flow out to the very limits of macrocosmic space – and such boundaries do exist... This vaporised substance radiates into vast expanses of the universe, but it returns in the forces of light and warmth. And as it returns from cosmic space, it spiritually surrounds, through the hierarches, a little child who can only crawl, and helps that child to stand upright and walk.*

It is possible then, with a stretch of our imagination, to see the forces and powers streaming out from fiery, volcanic Lemuria being returned to the earth and being made spiritually active through the hierarchies in order that we should gain our uprightness. We were, although certainly not in our physical outer appearance, as little children supported by the gods, as we came from our floating horizontal way of moving about to our earliest uprightness.

Through his clairvoyant observations Rudolf Steiner gives the following account:

> Humans were so different that one really hesitates to describe them... They had had more or less the development of an amphibian, a reptile, which was just beginning to breathe through lungs, and from the former floating, swimming motion, were learning little by little to raise and support themselves on earth... They had a mode of progression that alternated between a hop, scarcely to be called a step, and then a flight into the air... Nothing

_____

* Ibid.

remains to be discovered by the geologist as solidifications or fossils, for the body was quite soft; it contained as yet no kind of bony structure... The nearest comparison we could make is to the harder, but similar form of the Saurians.*

This was taking place just after the exit of the moon, from out of the relatively soft, volatile earth.

Thus in early Lemuria, the earth was a kind of fiery mass, in which the modern mineral was for the most part dissolved and fluid, as in an iron-foundry, and out of this developed the first mineral island masses. Upon these there wandered, half hopping, half hovering, the fore-parents of humanity... In later times there still continued a magical connection between human will and the forces of fire.†

In both his coloured pastel sketch and his black-and-white drawing of Lemuria, Rudolf Steiner depicts three small figures, semi-animal/reptilian forms, supporting themselves on three of the elevations rising up out of the earth below. These figures seem to be reaching out, straining upwards towards the forces streaming powerfully down towards them from the large profiles and beings above. They are early human forms striving towards uprightness.

---

* Rudolf Steiner, *Theosophy of the Rosicrucian*, Lecture 11.
† Ibid.

Chapter 11
The Influence of Angels and Luciferic Beings in Human Speech

'In self-forgetfulness
And mindful of its primal state
The growing human I
Speaks to the World-All:
If I can free myself
From fetters of my selfhood
In you, I establish my true being.'
– Rudolf Steiner, *Calendar of the Soul* (Verse 3)

Angelic beings, who are the great inspirers of humanity, and to whom the ancient Egyptians referred as their teachers, did not appear in physical human bodies. They could only manifest themselves through human beings. However, beings who were in a mid-position between humans and angels were still able, in very early times, to incarnate into human bodies.

Amongst the human race living on earth in Lemurian and Atlantean times, we find people whose innermost soul-nature was actually that of an angel in a backward state. Not only 'ordinary people' were going about the earth, but beings who only outwardly looked like them.

Beings belonging to the lowest category of luciferic individualities were actually present among humans. At the same times that angel beings were working into human civilisations through human beings, luciferic beings were also incarnated and were founding human civilisations in various places. When folk legends and mythology relate that in a particular place there lived a great person who was the founder of a civilisation, we can understand that such a being, a 'Lucifer being', was not necessarily the vehicle of evil, but rather that human civilisation was to receive countless blessings from them, bringing considerable advancements.

Individualisation, differentiation and freedom came from these beings – even the ability to speak a particular language rather than the uniform speech which once was spoken. This phase of development is described in the biblical Tower of Babel in Genesis.

In Lemurian times, there existed a kind of primitive human language which was the same all over the earth. Early humanity, when influenced by something outside of themselves, expressed this in a consonantal sound; an inner experience of the soul was given expression through vowel sounds. This speech was prompted in human souls by the inspiration of advanced human beings, who were very highly developed.

But in order that human beings could become more individualised, humankind had to be separated out of its unified existence. Different languages in different parts of the world are due to influences in which luciferic beings were incarnated. These spirits had formerly perfected their development during the earlier phase of moon evolution.

Harmonious, dreamlike unity was brought about in humanity through the influences of the angels and higher hierarchies; individuality and diversity were instigated through Lucifer beings who had a special mission in the future progress of humanity. On the one hand these were confusing and at times destructive impulses, which fragmented humankind. In Genesis, Chapter 11, we read:

> And the whole earth was of one language and of one speech. And as it came to pass they journeyed to the East, that they found a plain in the land of Shinar; and they dwelt there… And they said, Go to, let us build us a city and a tower whose top may reach to heaven; and let us make a name, lest we be scattered abroad upon the whole face of the earth.

And the Lord came down to see the city and the tower which the children of men built.

And the Lord said, Behold the people is one and they have all one language; and this they begin to do: and now nothing will be restrained from them, which they have imagined to do. Go to, let us go down and confound their language that they may not understand each other's speech. So the Lord scattered them abroad from there, upon the face of all the earth... Therefore is the name of it called Babel, because the Lord did confound the language of all the earth.

Although the Tower of Babel was constructed many thousands of years after the Lemurian times, during the second post-Atlantean epoch of Babylonia, influences springing from Lucifer originated in Lemuria with humanity's gradual descent from the spiritual worlds. Humanity yielded to the temptation of the luciferic serpent, to the allurement of a new consciousness, which the female human being had already approached. The Tower of Babel can be considered to have been a mighty physical structure built in a futile endeavour to ascend upwards towards the divine spiritual heights and pure radiance of heaven, now lost in the processes of humanity's descent, the Fall.

One unified language united early humanity and gave a human voice to the resounding harmony of the gods. Gradually it began to reflect the wrought world into which the human being, permeated by luciferic beings, was descending.

Before the descent, human bodies were composed of warmth and watery-air, moving about horizontally, intoning and resounding, creating great sound-waves and currents in their surrounding etheric world. As the luciferic beings entered into them, a gradual densification in their fluid constitution occurred, which in turn densified and contracted further into a more substantial, 'physical' body. Humans gradually became heavier, sinking down from the periphery to the surface of the earth.

'What was of universal dimension, the macrocosmic mystery, became the microcosmic mystery of human speech... And the whole world became speech.'* The cosmic word was active in the world-wisdom of Creation.

'Out of the ground [of the world] the Lord God formed every beast of the field and every bird of the air, and brought them to the human being to see what they would call them; and whatever the human being called every living creature, that was its name.'†

---

* Rudolf Steiner Mystery Knowledge and Mystery Centres. Lecture 6, 2 December 1923

† Genesis, 2: 19. See also Rudolf Steiner, *The Spiritual Guidance of the Individual and Humanity*, 2 June 1910 & 20 August 1911, and *Genesis, Secrets of the Bible Story of Creation*, 17-26 August 1910. Also, Emil Bock, *Genesis*, Chapter 2.

Chapter 12
Saving our Senses – Protection against Lucifer and Ahriman

'Into our inner being
Pour the riches of our senses.
The Cosmic Spirit finds itself
Reflected in the human eye
Which ever must renew itself
From that spirit source.'
– Rudolf Steiner, *Calendar of the Soul* (Verse 52)

We perceive the world around us through our senses, which in themselves function without our being consciously aware of them. Our senses function 'automatically', conveying a multitude of audible, visible, tactile and tangible impressions to us which relay information about our surroundings, unless any condition causes discomfort or impairment. We perceive the physical world because our senses are 'transparent', usually non-detectable, and we simply don't notice them, but only what they are conveying to us.

Rudolf Steiner spoke of them as being selfless,* and went on to say that if they were self-seeking, we would, for example, experience the colour blue with a sensation of suction in our eyes due to the nature of the colour blue itself. Blue recedes in colour perspective, it seems to fade away into cool distances. We could imagine how uncomfortable it would be if we felt as though our eyes were being gently pulled out from our eye-sockets by the blue colour – we could never gaze so appreciatively into a lovely blue sky! And more dramatically, the nature of red is to move forwards in colour space, to come

---

* Rudolf Steiner, Basel, 2 June 1914.

towards us. If we were conscious of our senses, we would experience red as a stabbing sensation in our eyes, and actually feel discomfort, even pain, depending on the intensity of the colour.

This was indeed the intention of Lucifer, to stimulate and bring consciousness into the senses. Having led us into the sense world during our gradual descent on to the earth, Lucifer desired to go further and to bring consciousness into the senses themselves, so that they would actually respond to outer stimuli.

But how were we protected from this taking place? Rudolf Steiner describes* how the being of Christ ensouled himself in one of the archangels, who offered up his own soul powers in order to be permeated by Christ. And this released a force which quietened and harmonised our senses. This was one aspect of Christ's pre-earthly deeds.

Gradually, humanity will come to realise that it is not only ourselves but Christ within our senses. And, slowly we will learn to develop deep feelings of gratitude and reverence as we experience and appreciate all the beauty of the natural world around us.

A further pre-earthly deed of Christ protected and guided our capacities to stand upright and to walk, which were acquired in slow stages during the Lemurian epoch.

As well as the influence of the fire element (outlined in Chapter 10), when *outer* forces connected to fire activity streamed in from the cosmos, the Spirits of Form, the Exusiai, or in Hebrew the Elohim, poured the first phase of the ego into the human being from out of their own substance.

This first manifestation of the 'I' was an *inner* force, by means of which human beings could raise themselves into an upright position. Both of the adversaries, Lucifer and Ahriman,

---

* Ibid.

would have been able to bring about disaster to the whole of humanity due to this upright position, which was removing human beings from the spiritual forces of the earth.* However, an angelic being in the etheric realm took on the form of an etheric human being and was able to stream his etheric forces, together with the forces of the sun, into the etheric bodies of humanity. This saved us from disastrous influences which would have otherwise entered into us from Lucifer and Ahriman.

Who was this angelic being? Rudolf Steiner informs us[†] that it was the future Nathan Jesus, Jesus of Nazareth, who was, during the time of Lemuria, an angelic being. The divine presence of Christ permeated the angelic Nathan Jesus, and enabled him to assume a human etheric form, thereby providing a divine protection for developing humanity. His etheric forces, permeated by Christ, could surround, penetrate and protect humanity's etheric bodies during this phase of walking in an upright position for the very first time. And this protection still surrounds all young children to this day and into the future, as they learn to stand upright and to walk.[‡]

---

* Rudolf Steiner, 'The Pre-Earthly Deeds of Christ', Pforzheim, 7 March 1914.
[†] Ibid.
[‡] Ibid.

'Lemuria' by Rudolf Steiner. Black and white pencil drawing

'Flame' by Gerard Wagner

PART FIVE

Chapter 13
Training Magicians – The Magical Male Will

'Everywhere the burning of the burning, the flame of the flame, pain and the shadow of pain, joy and the rapt breath of joy, flame of flame that, burning, destroyeth not, till the flame is no more!'
— Fiona Macleod, 'Fragments'

One goal of the Lemurians was developing the will, which was specifically a task and responsibility of men. Education of male children was wholly directed toward this. In our present time, we would find certain practices to be quite shocking. For example, boys were trained to endure physical pain, which was inflicted upon them through searing heat or body piercings.* They were tested through undergoing dangers or trials, and accomplishing feats of daring and courage. They even had to endure tortures. Many boys were left to suffer and die, and were regarded as not being worthy members of Lemurian society.

However, a few male children were born with an advanced capacity: that of being a magician. This talent was developed through training and focusing strength of will in order to penetrate the secrets of nature.

To understand these practices, we must remember how vastly different the consciousness and attitudes were at this

---

* Still practised in certain places today, for example walking over red-hot stones, or fire-walking in Hawaii.
We also see body-piercing as a fashion in many societies at present, although usually painlessly!

ancient, pre-historic time. Life and death were experienced quite differently than now. Sympathy, empathy and compassion have developed more recently, although we are nevertheless still capable of war, cruelties and inflicting suffering.

Towards the end of Lemuria, elaborately imposing and ornate buildings were constructed which were educational and scientific, in the sense of being 'institutions' of natural science. We could consider these as being the world's first universities. They were for the cultivation and development of divine wisdom and the penetration of the mysteries of nature. They were the first Mystery Temples.

These temple institutions were for men who, through discipline, had acquired the ability to overcome themselves to a great extent. These men learned to know and to control the forces of nature through direct contemplation of them. Their learning was such that the forces of nature could be transformed into forces of their own will. Such men felt as though this was a direct gift from universal spiritual powers. When they received this gift, they considered themselves to be servants, or servers, of these universal powers. They felt as though they were sanctified from everything unspiritual. Their tasks were sacred.

The religious mood and atmosphere was due to the men strictly guarding and protecting the powers given to them, as divine secrets. They lived sanctified or holy lives, and in their temples they actively participated in direct contemplation of nature's active forces. They were able to look into the spiritual creative workshop of nature, and could experience a communion with the beings which build the world itself. Rudolf Steiner called this communication, 'an association with the gods'.

Such men were few in number and were regarded with great awe and wonder by the average Lemurians, who were at a much lower stage of development, almost animalistic in nature. This veneration was due to the power and guidance which the more advanced or initiated men could exercise, and who, through their magical will, could guide and direct the development of humanity.

These men were born magicians and trained from an early age. Through their own self-discipline and dedication, they could be initiated into the science of universal laws and learning how to manage them, and thus become the trusted leaders of what would be a long, gradual and tumultuous development of the Lemurian phase of existence.

Chapter 14
Women and the Nature Mysteries – The Origin of Religion

'Day by day the wind-wings lifted a more multitudinous whisper from the woodlands. The deep hyperborean note, from the invisible ocean of air, was still audible…'

– Fiona Macleod 'Fragments'

Lemurian girls were trained in developing their imagination. This was done mainly through observing the powers and processes of nature. For example, the grandeur and dreadful powers of the great storms, which raged during these times, would be calmly observed, and this would fill a girl's soul with a deep appreciation for the strength and might of nature. Awe, wonder and respect would gradually develop into religious devotion.

Women who were trained in this way could then look into the creative workshop of nature, and communicate with the spiritual beings who were the builders of the world. They could commune with the gods, and thereby developed special human powers.

Their imaginative faculties became the basis for a higher development, that of the inner realm of ideas. They could absorb the forces of nature into themselves, which then had an after-effect in the soul, namely that the beginnings of memory were being formed; and with memory, the capacity to form the earliest and simplest moral concepts could come about.

In this way, it was through women that the first ideas of good and evil arose. They could love and value some of the things which had made a good and positive impression on their imaginative awareness, and dislike or even be revolted by other impressions. Women could interpret the forces of nature through inner reflection, and this in turn would become a foundation of morality.* Females could access spiritual powers through feeling – through a sense of divinity in the feelings that they could experience in their soul.

Also, through their memory-faculties, women had acquired the capacity to make experiences of the past useful for the future. This enabled them to guide and direct small groups or communities, and to refine the vigorous, wilful strength of the men. The influence of women was quite considerable in community life. In a dreamlike contemplative manner, they could sense and interpret the secrets of nature, which guided their actions, and in turn those of the community.

All of nature, everything around them, was animated, full of life and pulsing with living energies. They could 'hear' the sounding, the speaking of animals, plants, stones, water, wind and the weather. They could understand the wind whispering in the trees, the sounds of gurgling, running water, singing birds, the passing clouds and the falling rain. Nature revealed itself and spoke its wisdom. Women could abandon themselves in trance-like states to receive nature's guidance. They were consulted for advice and for interpretation of natural events in order to support and strengthen communal life.

The spiritual in nature and within human life gradually came to be worshipped and venerated. A sense that all life was sacred developed initially through the more highly advanced women, and then into the communities they influenced. Some women attained a special pre-eminence due to their being able, through the mysterious depths of their own soul-life, to interpret world-secrets. In a sense, these soul capacities were the origin of religious feelings.

Eventually, such women could transpose their feelings into a natural language as an expression of what they felt inwardly.

---

* *Cosmic Memory*, 'The Lemurian Race'.

Rudolf Steiner indicates that the beginning of language lies in something which is similar to song.* The inner life of soul became audible. All of nature's voices and rhythms sounded through these wise women. People would gather around them to hear their songlike chanting and sounding, and felt as though higher powers were speaking through these women. In this way, human worship of the gods began.

_____

* Ibid.

Chapter 15
Hearing the Gods

'Thus speaks the cosmic Word
That I by grace through senses' portals
Have led into my inmost soul:
"Imbue your spirit depths
With my wide world-horizons
To find in future time
Myself in you."'
– Rudolf Steiner, *Calendar of the Soul* (Verse 17)

The capacity of hearing was one of our earliest senses to develop. This came about through the tone ether of the cosmic Word, resounding through the universe like the humming, sighing 'sound of the sea'.

We could 'hear' with our whole being what lived as sound in the cosmos. Our sense of sound, or hearing, gives to us the knowledge about the objects and events of the outer world; it is the soul, the substance of the thing itself, which vibrates inside us and 'speaks' to us as sound. In our present time we perceive the vibrations of the air as sound. The etheric human being experienced the vibrations of the etheric matter which surrounded them. In this distant time, spiritual hearing gave us the experiences of hearing the music of the spheres, the 'sounding' of the spiritual hierarchies.

In *Occult Science* Rudolf Steiner writes:

> In the Sun time [i.e. the phase of evolution known as Ancient Sun], human beings abandoned themselves to the enjoyment of a kind of sun-life. They were lifted away from their own lives and lived more spiritually... They felt the very forces of the universe, as if all their influences were streaming into them, pulsating through them. They felt intoxicated

by the cosmic harmonies in which they could participate. During these times, the astral body was in a way freed from the 'physical', as was part of the life body (or etheric body), and these became as though a delicate and wonderful musical instrument upon which the cosmic mysteries resounded... shaping and moulding them in accordance with the harmonies of the universe. For in these harmonies, the beings of the sun were working, so that the astral and etheric bodies of humans were formed by the tones of spiritual, cosmic sound.

Much later, humans could sense within the sensations of warmth and sound, in their streaming and surging around them, the presence of the archai and archangels. They could not directly perceive these higher beings, but images of them arose within their souls when they were experiencing streams of warmth and sounds around them.

In two phases preceding the Lemurian, known as the Polarean and Hyperborean, human beings are described in theosophical terminology as the first two 'root races' of our earth. Gradually during these phases, the sense of hearing was no longer experienced through the whole human form. A special part of the 'body' remained capable of reverberating to delicate vibrations which provided the substance, or material, from which our present organs of hearing gradually developed.

In early Lemurian times, before the processes of descent occurred, early humanity experienced the sounding of the hierarchies in a dreamlike consciousness. As the inner soul-life developed, the soft malleable body adapted its shapes and forms to this inner life.

Much later, after the gradual descent onto the still volatile earth, groups began to diversify. Some were influenced by their regional and climatic surroundings, where hearing became outwardly oriented. Sensitively attuned to the sounds of nature all around them, they could hear nature resounding to them as a symphony of magical and powerful mystery. They absorbed in their souls the power of what they heard: the mysterious depths of what the world contained.

However, in these early times they did not have language in the true sense. They vocalised natural sounds in response to the inner feelings of pleasure and joy, discomfort and pain. These later became what we would term vowel sounds, and were expressions of their inner life. Humans' hearing of the world around them was expressed through the inner feelings which this evoked, rather than naming or designating external objects. We hear such sounds in babies and young infants who give at times very clear indications of their inner condition – although perhaps more in crying than expressing their joys.

The experiences of girls and women developed into inner capacities of dreamy imagination, which was highly valued and was stimulated through events in the natural world. As the gods created all that took place in the realms of nature, it could be said that they dreamed nature. And so, in turn, were these processes and forms able to penetrate into the female soul: they dreamed the dreams of the gods.

Towards the end of Lemuria, society became more defined. Some women advanced to becoming priestesses, who were able to be inspired by the higher guides of humanity in order to direct and protect the course of human development.

Certain tones and rhythms were given to the priestesses who were advanced enough to hear them in mystic communion, and were inspired to sing and chant these tones. This would, in turn, enable, awaken and uplift the souls of their attentive listeners. This was really the beginning of human worship of the gods, which has continued through thousands of years, being expressed by the signing of songs of exultation and praise, the devout and reverent saying of prayers and the reciting of 'mantric verse'.

Are we not now inwardly moved by listening to a magnificent symphony, or an uplifting piece of choral music, or a humanly complex and moving opera? We could wonder whether composers were and are still inspired by higher beings who wish and need to make their presence felt within our souls? We do know that many composers have acknowledged hearing the sacred sounding of the natural world as the starting point for their musical inspiration.

We can question: Are we still hearing nature or the gods – and which gods are we listening to now?

'Lemuria' by Rudolf Steiner. Pastel sketch

PART SIX

Chapter 16
Isis and Osiris – The Sun and the Moon

'In the beginning when God began to create the heavens and the earth, the earth was without form and void, and darkness was upon the face of the deep; and the Spirit of God was moving over the face of the waters'

– Genesis 1: 1-3

Osiris reigned as the great God of the Sun, when mists and vapours still covered the earth, and there was as yet no air, no breath and no conscious experience of death for humanity, whose lower nature was rooted within the water, half-sunk into the dark water-earth. There was no firm human shape, but a flower-like form which continuously metamorphosed itself.

But as the sun separated itself from the earth more and more, and as the vapour sphere, which was the realm of humanity's higher nature, became more refined, human beings were able to gradually perceive the direct influence of the sun less and less. They could increasingly acquire a consciousness of their lower nature, reaching a stage where the ego could be experienced.

However, Osiris was the great spirit being who contained the force of the sunlight in such a way that when the moon departed from the earth, he accompanied it. He then received the task of reflecting sunlight from the moon to the earth. But the light of the sun reflected by the moon is different every night and day, as the moon goes through its phases, fourteen waxing – the full-moon – followed by fourteen waning, and no moon.

Osiris takes on fourteen forms, fourteen phases of growth in order to guide the light of the sun to us. These are the fourteen pieces of the dismembered Osiris, and the complete Osiris is the full moon. During the fourteen days and nights leading to the new moon, there is, however, no influence from Osiris. Rather, these phases are ruled by Isis.

This is not merely symbolic, but deeply connected to the human constitution. Where do we find twenty-eight pairs of nerves? In the spinal column, where we actually have thirty-one pairs of spinal nerves. There would have been twenty-eight had the moon-year coincided with the sun-year. But the sun-year is longer, and this difference caused the surplus nerves.

The duality of male and female first occurred through this alternating influence of Isis and Osiris from the moon sphere. An organism in which the Isis influence predominated was male, whereas a body in which the Osiris influence prevailed became female. Both forces work in every male and female, but in such a way that the male has a female etheric body, and the female has a male etheric body.

Through the influences that proceed from sun and moon, the masculine and feminine principles are regulated: in every female, something masculine e.g. the larynx; in every male, something female, e.g. the lungs.

Gradually, the human being could move out of the horizontal and become vertical. This occurred through the influence of Isis and Osiris: the balancing of sun and moon. The tempo of evolution, however, can be measured by the sun moving through the whole zodiac, and it was only after a complete circuit of 25,920 years that a forward step in evolution could be completed.

> And God said, 'Let there be light', and there was light. And God saw that the light was good; and God separated the light from the darkness. God called the light Day, and the darkness he called Night. And there was evening and there was morning, one day.*

---

* Genesis 1: 3-5. See also Rudolf Steiner, *Egyptian Myths and Mysteries*, 8 September 1908.

Chapter 17
Isis and Osiris

'A mist went up from the earth and watered the whole face of the ground – then the Lord God formed man of dust from the ground and breathed into his nostrils the breath of life; and man became a living being.'

– Genesis 2: 6-8

The festival of Osiris was celebrated in Egypt on 6 January as a celebration of Isis re-finding Osiris after his being overcome and dismembered by his brother, Typhon. Also celebrated among the Assyrians, Armenians and Phoenicians, it was a festival of rebirth from out of the water. Isis, his consort and widow, twice sought far and wide for her missing husband, Osiris, who as the Sun God had long ruled the earth, to the great blessing of humanity.

His light-filled influence was powerful up to a certain time, characterised later as the period when the sun stood in the star sign of Scorpio (the scorpion). It was then that Osiris was killed by Typhon (or Set) who persuaded him to lie down in a chest, which became his coffin. Typhon closed the chest and cast Osiris into the sea. This chest was the moon, being pushed out into cosmic space as it withdrew from the earth.

Isis searched for him and, after finding him (in the region of Phoenicia), raised him out of the water and brought him to Egypt. But Typhon cut him into fourteen pieces, which Isis then gathered and buried in fourteen different places. She later gave birth to Horus, her divine son, who avenged his father.

Osiris once again entered into the world of the divine spiritual beings. No longer directly active on earth, he aided human beings on their journey in the spiritual worlds between death and rebirth. The fourteen aspects of the moon are the fourteen pieces of the dismembered Osiris. Within this ancient Egyptian myth, and in its festive celebratory rituals, lies hidden a mighty cosmic event.

The two brothers were experienced as light-Osiris, and air-Typhon. As long as humanity experienced only light, death was unknown. Before the middle of the Lemurian epoch, no human being could breathe air. They felt themselves to be eternal, and united with their watery surroundings. In the biblical sense, 'the Spirit of God brooded over the waters'.

With the first drawing of breath, the awareness of birth and death entered into human consciousness. The 'air-breath' Typhon had separated from his brother Osiris, 'light-ray'. Typhon was the air-breath that had brought mortality to humanity.

But what did the disappearance of Osiris signify? It marked an important transition from the epoch before the middle of Lemuria to the epoch after. In early Lemurian times, humanity was not warm-bloodied and could be likened to fishes, in the sense that their own warmth and the warmth of the environment were equal in degree. Sometime around the middle of the Lemurian epoch, the descent of manas, or spirit-self, was disseminated from the spiritual worlds into humanity.

In each single human being, a 'grave' was created so that the dismembered Osiris could dwell within human bodies. In the Egyptian mystery-language, human bodies were called 'the graves of Osiris'. This brought about the nature of desire, or passion, into Lemurian humanity.

For the first time, humanity became warm-blooded and gradually began to solidify. The upper part of the physical body slowly transformed so that it could take in air, and with the air, divine forces streamed into it. The human being was beginning to become a self-forming, self-contained being. Through diving down into their own lower nature, human beings could become conscious of themselves for the first time. And they became naked in the sight of God.*

* See Rudolf Steiner, *Egyptian Myths and Mysteries*, lectures of 7 & 8 September 1908, and *The Festivals and their Meaning*, 30 December 1904.

Chapter 18
The Question of Time

'And God said, let there be lights in the firmament of the heavens to divide the day from the night; and let there be signs for seasons, and for days and years.'

— Genesis 1: 14-15

In a lecture given in 1905, Rudolf Steiner mentioned a specific time-period – 'The Lemurian age lasted twenty-two million years' – and that the reversal of the earth's axis required perhaps four million years. He had also spoken about the etheric human form not being differentiated from that of the etheric group soul of animals as being, 'millions of years in the past'.

Regarding earth's geology he outlined: 'If we go back some thousands of years in Europe we find Europe covered in ice; if we go back millions of years, we find in the same regions a tropical climate.'* And in a further example: '…millions of years ago there were vast fern forests in regions where coal is today'. The human form was created, Steiner explained, from the activities of the hierarchies, in particular Spirits of Form, the Exusiai, originating in the zodiac.†

As the spring equinox moved through the twelve constellations, one aspect of the human 'body' was created in turn, beginning with the feet, when the spring equinox stood in Pisces, during early Lemuria. We must remember, however, how different the human form was at this time, the 'feet' being appendages which enabled the human being – whose form was mainly etheric substance only – to move through the watery environment.

---

* Rudolf Steiner, *Foundations of Esotericism*, 25 October 1905.
† See *Egyptian Myths and Mysteries*, 9, 10 & 11 September 1908.

A complete cycle through the whole zodiac is known as a cosmic year, taking 25,920 years, and each new step in the creation of the human form sometimes required several complete cycles before the next step could be completed. Rudolf Steiner explained:

> Therefore we cannot apply to more ancient times the familiar time-reckonings of post-Atlantean epochs. The sun had first to go completely around – in earlier ages even several times – before evolution could progress a step. For those parts [of the human being] that required a stronger moulding [e.g. for the hip region which occurred when the sun was in the sign of the Balance, the Scales], the time needed was even longer. Human beings rise ever higher through this evolution. The next stage, during which the lower parts of the human trunk were formed, is designated by the sign of the Virgin.*

This cosmic aspect of time brings earthly and human evolution into relationship with the working of spiritual beings. It is interesting to note that in his remarkable and complex book *Occult Science, An Outline*, describing the spiritual evolution of earth and humanity in great detail, not a single date is mentioned. It is as though Rudolf Steiner entered into a timeless realm as he perceived the magnificent spiritual images of the Akashic Record. Time was held within a pictorial space, realms where 'time and space become one'.

However, when he attempted to express his research in terms of time, by his own admission this was extremely difficult, and he made huge efforts to translate his spiritual observations into everyday language. It is helpful to remember that before the sun, moon and earth were all separated in various stages throughout long eons of time, time itself was very different to what it is at present. It was actually only after the

---

* Ibid., 10 September 1908.

moon departed from the earth that the seasonal and day/night rhythms were established.

It all remains somewhat mysterious – somehow 'veiled in the mists of time' – until we realise that time, space and our own existence are held within the consciousness of mighty spiritual beings. We could say that all that exists within the course of time is being created and sustained by the hierarchies. Here we step into the realm of the spirit and in particular to the Elohim, who Rudolf Steiner says are identified with the exalted spiritual beings of the second hierarchy, known in Christian terminology as Exusiai, Powers or Spirits of Form. Their thinking is so advanced that through it they are actually forming and creating existence. They were active throughout the Saturn, Sun and Moon evolutionary phases, creating and bringing order, and remain active during Earth evolution.

After bringing light into existence, they appointed the Time Spirits, the archai (the Principalities or Spirits of Personality) to continue and sustain their creative work. These mighty Time Spirits are creating 'Time Intervals', and it is the first Time Spirit who is hidden within the customary biblical phrase in Genesis, 'the first day'.

The original Hebraic word 'yom' is usually translated as 'day'. However, the Gnostics referred to the spiritual powers, or spiritual beings, who entered into the unfolding of existence, as Aeons, beings guiding development in succession, one taking over from another. An Aeon is a being, a living entity, and it was only much later that the abstract concept of time was associated with the word Aeon.

In the Aryan languages, we find a connection between the words 'dues' and 'dies' – God and day. And perhaps also in our English term for God – the Deity – and also in 'deities', referring to the Gods. So, we can reinterpret the original 'yom' as not referring to our modern concept of a 24-hour day.

Rather, 'yom' as 'day' is actually a spiritual being, an Archai or Time-Spirit. The expression in Genesis, 'let them be for signs and for seasons and for days and years', can be understood as the Archai serving the Elohim, sustaining their creation as mighty beings of Time.

And how can we understand the night? 'And God called the light 'day' and the darkness He called Night.' The rhythmic, regular interplay of day and night are essential for our existence. During the night we are refreshed and renewed during our sleep, as our astral body and 'I' journey out into starry realms. Who, then, created and is creating the night?

If we look back to the earliest stage of our earth, the time of Ancient Saturn, there was warmth but no light. Existence was entirely made up of warmth ether. Then, during the following phase of existence, the Ancient Sun, light ether radiated into the darkness and the warmth. We read in Genesis: 'And God [the Elohim] said, "Let there be light", and there was light.'

The Ancient Sun was an interweaving of light, warmth and air, and a fluctuating shadow of darkness, created by Archai who remained behind in their Saturn phase of development. It is the more slowly advancing Saturn Archai who are active in us when we are asleep, renewing our physical and etheric bodies. They are the Time Sprits and are also active as the Spirits of the Age in earth's evolution.

The various names given to time, to the day and the night in earlier civilisations, are indeed a cultural folk-memory of this knowledge. When we are in time, we are indeed within mighty spiritual beings, the Archai, who are time itself, bestowing their sublime cosmic presence upon us.

Rudolf Steiner says that:

> …the Spirits of Wisdom became the Spirits of the Rotation of Times. The successive incarnations of humans were regulated in the successive revolutions of time, which were

in turn regulated through the course of the stars. They, the Spirits of Wisdom, would have been able to lift humanity away from the earth by their wisdom-filled power, but then humanity would have had to forego the maturing of the fruits of love, of earthly experience, which can only take place in the course of time…

The Spirits of Wisdom, at the very beginning of earthly evolution, in the Lemurian age, would have taken human beings away out of the body, led them to a rapid spiritual evolution and quickly consumed their bodies, in which case the Earth could have never fulfilled its mission … So, a balance is held between the Spirits of Form and the Spirits of Light who have become the Spirits of the Rotation of Time.*

_____

* *The Influence of Spiritual Beings Upon Man*, Berlin, 24 March 1908. See also Rudolf Steiner, *Genesis. Secrets of the Bible Story of Creation*, 17-26 August 1910.

'Spirit Seed' by Gerard Wagner

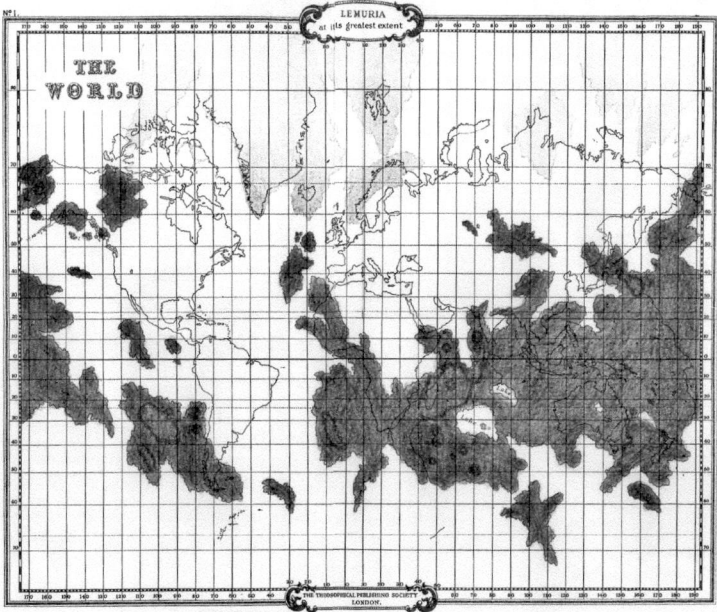

'Lemuria at its greatest extent' by W. Scott-Elliot

PART SEVEN

Chapter 19
The Enthusiasts of the Nineteenth Century

'And God said "Let the waters under the heavens be gathered together in one place, and let the dry land appear." And it was so. God called the dry land Earth, and the waters that were gathered together he called Seas.
And God saw that it was good.'

— Genesis: 1-9

The South Sea at one time formed a large Pacific Continent, and the numerous little islands which now lie scattered in it, were simply the highest peaks of the mountains covering that continent. The Indian Ocean formed a continent which extended from the Sunda Islands along the southern coast of Asia to the east coast of Africa. This large continent of former times, Sclater, an Englishman, has called Lemuria, from the monkey-like animals, the Lemurs, which inhabited it.*

Philip Sclater (1829–1913), secretary of the Zoological Society for over forty years, was one of the great pioneering bio-geographers who specialised in animal distribution. Widely travelled through the Americas, India, Madagascar and Australia, he questioned how it was possible for Lemur fossils to have been found in both Madagascar and India, which were separated by the vast Indian Ocean.

He surmised that at one time dry land must have connected the two and wrote:

> The anomalies of the mammal fauna of Madagascar can best be explained by supposing that a large continent

---

* William Scott-Elliot, *The Story of Atlantis and the Lost Lemuria.*

occupied parts of the Indian Ocean … broken up into islands of which some have become amalgamated with Africa, some with what is now Asia, and that in Madagascar and the Mascarene islands (Reunion, Mauritius and Rodrigues) we have existing relics of this great continent, for which I propose the name Lemuria.*

The nineteenth century saw a considerable flurry of excitement and interest in this mysterious continent of Lemuria. Geologists, botanists, archaeologists and anthropologists of that time pounced eagerly on each new discovery in order to fit the earth's great jig-saw puzzle together. Debates were held, hypotheses put forward, papers were presented, and each new find proved further convincing evidence that Lemuria was no mere fable but indeed existed in all its exotic and remarkable aspects. Courageous expeditions and painstaking research revealed that the earth had indeed, throughout millions of years, undergone extraordinary geological changes.

Ernst Haeckel, in his great work *The History of Creation*, had written: 'neither Australia, nor America, nor Europe can have been this primeval home [of humanity], or the so-called "Paradise", the cradle of the human race'. He continued:

Most circumstances indicate southern Asia as the locality in question, and the only other of the now existing continents which may be considered is Africa. But there are a number of circumstances (especially chorological facts) which suggest that the primeval home of humanity was a continent now sunk beneath the surface of the Indian Ocean, which extended along the south of Asia, as it is at present, and probably connected to it, extending eastwards as far as Further India and the Sunda Islands;

---

* From 'Searching for Lemuria', Maarten Ekama, *New View* magazine, Summer 2017.

towards the west, as far as Madagascar and the south-east shores of Africa… By assuming this Lemuria to have been the primeval home of humanity, we facilitate the explanation of the geographical distribution of the human species by migration.*

The learned natural scientists of the time thoroughly examined all the available proofs of this bygone age. The work of Isidore Geoffroy Saint-Hilaire, Dr Hartlaub, Dr Stoliezka, Andrew Murray, Mr Searles, V. Wood, Professors Huxley and Ramsay, Mr Woodward and Mr Tate, were some of the leading exponents of natural research during the nineteenth century, and references to their work are included in W. Scott-Elliot's *The Lost Lemuria*.

Significant publications elucidated the plant and animal kingdoms, for example Henry Blandford's article, 'On the age and correlations of the plant-bearing series of India and the former existence of an Indo-Oceanic Continent', published in the *Quarterly Journal of the Geological Society*, Vol. 31, in 1875. Henry's brother, William, was one of the first geologists to realise that fossils were actually a record of a region's geological history. The brothers discovered evidence of glaciers in sub-tropical India's distant past, a revolutionary discovery at the time. Also of note was A.R. Wallace's *The Geographical Distribution of Animals – with a study of the relations of living and extinct faunas as elucidating the past changes of the earth's surface*, published in 1876 by Macmillan and Co. in London.

Eduard Suess (1831–1914), a member of the Austrian Parliament and a highly respected professor of both Palaeontology and Geology at the University of Vienna, had introduced

---

* Paraphrased from Ernst Haeckel, *The History of Creation*, Vol. II, pp. 325-6. Quoted in William Scott-Elliot, *The Story of Atlantis and the Lost Lemuria.*

the idea of the earth's biosphere. He wrote extensively on his ideas on the earth's cooling and contracting in his four-volume work, *The Face of the Earth*. He gathered data from South Africa, the Arabian Peninsula, India, Australia and South America to prove the existence of a continent, now no longer in existence, which he named Gondwanaland after an area in the east Deccan part of central India, which was once home to an aboriginal tribe, the Gonds.

The scientist Alfred Wegener (1880–1930), a courageous explorer, put forward the possibility of continental drift, presenting his ideas in a lecture at the Geological Society in Frankfurt in 1912. He drew attention to the many affinities of fossils and rocks on opposite sides of the Atlantic, and the matching coastlines of both continents. He published detailed research in his book *Die Enstehung der Kontinente und Ozeane* ('The Origins of the Continents and Oceans'), explaining that the continents move slowly over vast periods of time. He suggested that, over 300 million years ago, they had all been joined together in a vast continent which he named Pangaea.

It is interesting to note that Rudolf Steiner had a copy of Wegener's book in his own library. He had explained to the Waldorf teachers in Stuttgart that continents floated in the deep, more fluid layers of the earth, and that their positioning is determined by the constellations and not by earthly forces.

We can be both fascinated and impressed by the thoroughness and detail of the nineteenth century investigations of the physical proof of Lemuria, but not forget that spiritual insights were also given at this time by H.P. Blavatsky, followed in the early twentieth century by Rudolf Steiner in his books *Cosmic Memory* (1904), and his all-encompassing *Occult Science* (1910).

In a lecture entitled 'What has Geology to say about the Origin of the World?'* he acknowledged the significance of geologists' discoveries and outlined their work in some detail, particularly the work of Eduard Suess. He anticipated that the thoroughness of geological research would eventually support his own spiritual-scientific research.

---

* Given in Berlin, 9 February 1911. (German catalogue number 60 – not published in English.)

Chapter 20
The Maps

'...Lemuria stretched south of our present Asia, as far as Africa and Australia. This was the continent inhabited by our ancestors when they were Lemurians... The ground under their feet was most unsteady. Fire eruptions, volcanic powers, continually upheaved it. Ancient Lemuria was a kind of fire country.'
– Rudolf Steiner, *Theosophy and Rosicrucianism*, Lecture 10

In *The Lost Lemuria* Scott-Elliot wrote:

> We were told that it was by mighty Adepts in the days of Atlantis that the Atlantean maps were produced, but we are not aware whether the Lemurian maps were fashioned by some of the divine instructors in the days when Lemuria still existed, or in still later days of the Atlantean epoch... In the former case there was a globe, a good bas-relief in terracotta, and a well-preserved map on parchment, or skin of some sort, to copy from. In the present case [i.e. Lemuria] there was only a broken terracotta model and a very badly preserved and crumpled map, so that the difficulty of carrying back the remembrances of all the details, and consequently of reproducing exact copies, has been far greater.

Unfortunately, Scott-Elliot provides us with almost no information regarding the sources of these maps. He writes, in *The Story of Atlantis* only the briefest of references: '...there are maps of the world at various periods of its history and it has been the great privilege of the writer to be allowed to obtain copies – more or less complete – of four of these. All four represent Atlantis and the surrounding lands at different epochs of their history'. He then continues with detailed descriptions of these particular maps, their geological aspects and time-spans.

The first of these four maps include references to Lemuria. I paraphrase: The first map represents the land surface of the earth as it existed about a million years ago, when the Atlantean 'race' was at its height, and before the great submergence took place around 800,000 years ago. The continent of Atlantis extended from a few degrees east of Iceland to the site now occupied by Rio de Janeiro in South America, embracing Texas and the Gulf of Mexico, eastern America, up to and including Labrador, stretched across to Scotland, Ireland and a small portion of the north of England. Its equatorial lands embraced Brazil and the whole stretch of ocean to the African Gold Coast. Scattered fragments of what eventually became the continents of Europe, Africa and America, as well as remains of the still older, and once widespread continent of Lemuria, are also shown on this map. The remains of the still older Hyperborean continent, which was inhabited by the second 'root race', are also given. To quote directly from Scott-Elliot:

> On a second map, the catastrophe of 800,000 years ago caused very great changes in the land distribution of the globe... The dimensions of the remains of Lemuria have been further curtailed, while Europe, Africa and America have received accretions of territory.

Later, in *The Lost Lemuria* he wrote:

> The author has been privileged to obtain copies of two maps, one representing Lemuria (and the adjoining lands) during the period of that continent's greatest expansion, the other exhibiting its outlines after its dismemberment by great catastrophes, but long before its final destruction. It was never professed that the maps of Atlantis were correct to a single degree of latitude or longitude, but, with the far greater difficulty of obtaining the information in the present

case, it must be stated that still less must these maps of Lemuria be taken as absolutely accurate.

He continues later with his own descriptions:

But not even geological epochs are assigned to the maps… It would seem probable that the older of the two Lemurian maps represented the earth's configuration from the Permian, through the Triassic and into the Jurassic epoch, while the second map probably represents the earth's configuration through the Cretaceous and into the Eocene period. From the older of the two maps it may be seen that the equatorial continent of Lemuria at the time of its greatest extension nearly circled the globe…

A remarkable feature of the second map is the great length, and at parts the extreme narrowness, of the two great blocks of land into which the continent had by this time been split. The straits at present existing between the islands of Bali and Lombok coincide with a portion of the straits which then divided these two continents, and these straits continued in a northerly direction by the west. Our present land areas of Australia, New Zealand, Madagascar, parts of Somaliland, the south of Africa and the southern part of Patagonia are lands which have probably existed through all the intervening catastrophes since the early days of Lemuria. This also includes southern India and Ceylon [now Sri Lanka]. Japan is shown by the maps to have been above water, whether as an island or as part of a continent, since the date of the second Lemurian map. Spain too has doubtless existed since that time, and together with the northern parts of Norway and Sweden, is probably the oldest land in Europe. Great Britain and Northern Ireland, have been repeatedly connected with the European continent and repeatedly separated from it. This we know from the many geological layers and geographical changes which have taken place over millennia.

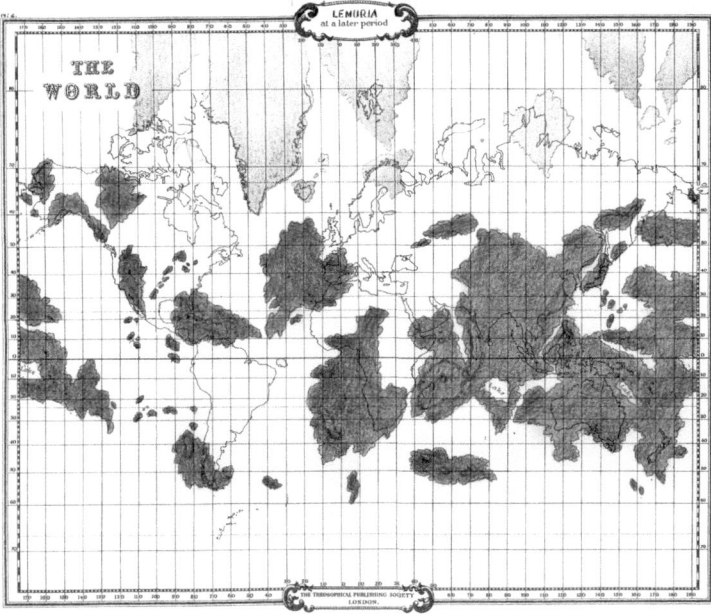

*From The Story of Atlantis and the Lost Lemuria by
W. Scott-Elliot*

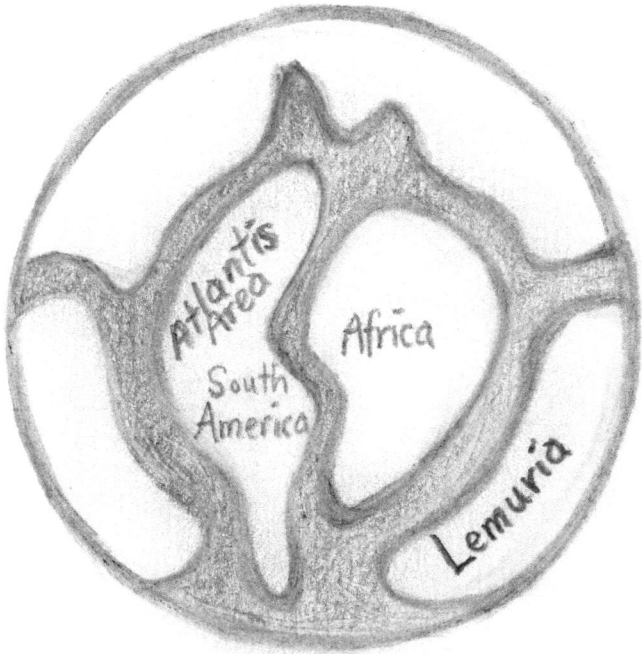

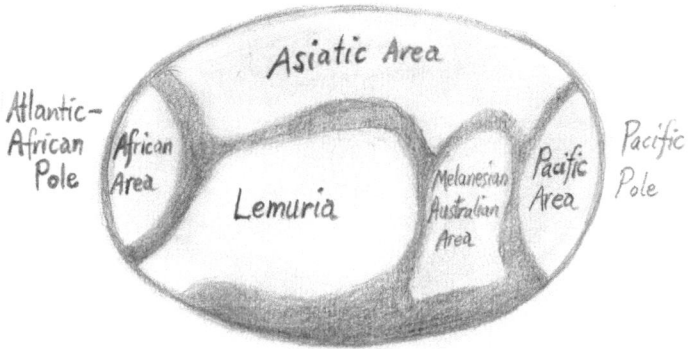

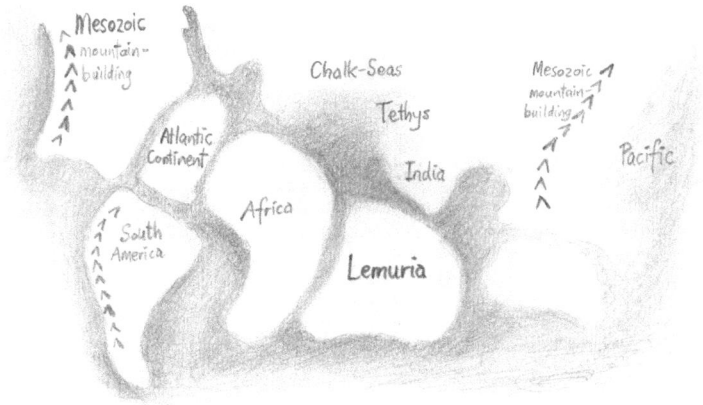

Maps attributed to Gunther Wachsmuth. Redrawn by the author

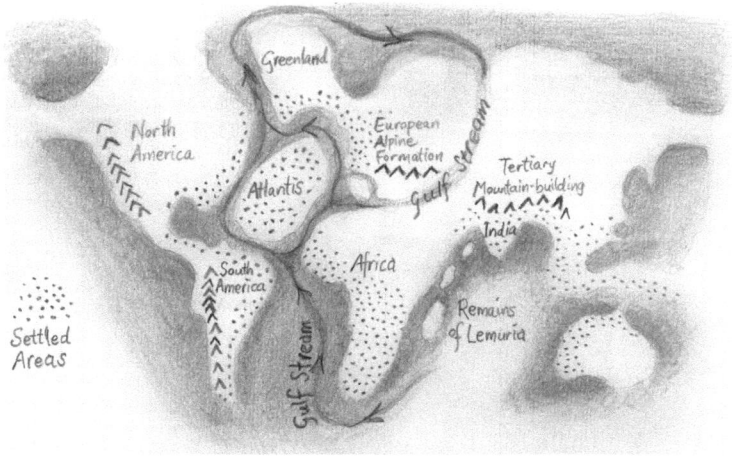

Maps attributed to Gunther Wachsmuth. Redrawn by the author

APPENDIX
Excerpts from *The Foundations of Esotericism* by Rudolf Steiner

'At the beginning of Genesis, when the Bible speaks of the human being, it speaks of a pure human being who is pure in the sense that they can bring forth their own being, called Adam Kadmon, and had nothing of the desire nature within them. The astral desire first appeared after they had incorporated other elements into themselves.

'Thus to begin with we have the pure human being who, up to the Lemurian age, actually led a supersensible existence and brought forth out of themselves everything that lived and was part of themselves. They hovered above what was manifested.

'At first the pure human being had found no means of incarnating on the earth. From among the huge powerful beings – strange gigantic beings, the animals – the human being made use of the most developed in order to incarnate in them. By attaching themselves to these animals, humans could bring into them their own astral body, which was in the heart, in the warm blood and in the circulation of the blood.

'Some animals whose descendants still exist today, such as sloths, kangaroos, beasts of prey, monkeys and apes, remained behind on the way. Everything in them which is of the desire nature (*kama*) was unloaded into them by the developing human beings. For example, rage was cast out into the lion, cunning into the fox. But these were purified by human beings in a process of purification leading upwards and becoming ennobled to the higher self, called by the Pythagoreans the process of catharsis. And spirit is now directed towards the animals in the form of elemental beings. Certain aspects of the animal-nature which originated from the human being, through the spirit of humanity, are now originating from elemental beings.

'By the last third of the Lemurian age, the human being had developed their physical, etheric and astral bodies, and had absorbed the plans, the directions and the laws which create life.'*

*

'At that time, human-beings had a very different physical, etheric and astral constitution. They went on all fours, sometimes standing and making a kind of leaping movement, having some slight power of using both their front limbs for grasping.

'The earth was inhabited by beings reptilian in character; human bodies too were reptile-like. When eventually this reptilian human being assumed an upright posture, the formation of the head was quite open in front, out of which gushed a fiery cloud. This gave rise to the tales about the winged serpent, the dragon, and such was the human being's grotesque form at that time.

'… The astral body with the head formation united with the winged-serpent body with its fiery opening. It was the fructification of the maternal earth with the paternal spirit. The lower astral body merged with the higher astral body, and a large part of the astral body then fell away. This part that fell away was bound up with the form of the winged-serpent and could no longer have any further development on the earth. It formed, as a conglomerate substance, the astral sphere of the moon, the so-called Eighth Sphere. The moon actually provides shelter for astral beings which have come into existence through the fact that humanity has thrown something off.

---

* From the lecture given in Berlin, 1 October 1905.

'At this time there were seven kinds or classes of human forms, differing somewhat from each other, from the finest, a highly-developed formation of the human form, down to those which were utterly grotesque. Our physical body has arisen through a transformation and ennobling of the serpent-like body from the Lemurian age.'*

*

'In the middle of the Lemurian age we find the first Sons of the Fire Mist; these incarnated in the fiery element, which at that time surrounded the earth. The sons of the Fire Mist were the first Arhats [perfected persons], they were angels in human form and could not go astray. Then there arose two other kinds.

'In the first Lemurian human race, those who had received only a small spark of the descending monad, the ego, were little adapted to forming a civilisation and soon went under. Those who had received nothing found expression for their lower nature and mingled with the animals. From them proceeded the last Lemurian races. The wild animal instincts lived in wild animal-like forms, which brought about a degeneration of the entire human substance through intermingling. It was then that the seed of karma was planted. Everything that came about later is the result of this original karma.

'However, certain monads, human egos in the highest sense, waited before incarnating. Through this the principle of ascetism entered into the world – reluctance to inhabit the earth and to enter into the sense experiences. The discrepancy between the higher and lower nature of the human being arose at this time. Because of it, humanity oscillates from one experience to another and further karma has come about.

---

* From the lecture given in Berlin, 16 October 1905.

'… The principle that leads the earth and evolution towards spirituality is Lucifer. Humanity must descend on to the earth, and to love the earth. Lucifer is the prince who reigns in the kingdoms of art and science, but his power does not suffice to allow him to descend altogether onto the earth and to lead it upwards. For this, a Sun adept is necessary, one who embraces the universality of human life, and this adept, a Sun Hero, is the Christ.'*

---

* From the lecture given in Berlin, 25 October 1905.

TIME CHART   **EPOCHS OF EVOLUTION**

Purely spiritual existence

Condensation as far as warmth-filled   Polarian
air.

Condensation as far as air and warmth   Hyperborean
(gas)

Separation of the earth-moon and the
sun

Geology begins

Pre-Cambrian	Thin liquid imbued with air and warmth. Gradual conden-sation of metals into liquids. Human being invisible; cloud-like.	Archaeon Early Lemurian (No fossil remains)
Cambrian	Foamy, jelly-like condition of the earth. Soft, mallea-ble human beings.	
Ordovician	Paleozoic	Primary Middle Lemurian (fishes)
Silurian	(Paleolithic)	
Devonian		
Carboniferous	30,000 BC	
Permian	Gradual Solidifica-tion of the earth	

Differentiation and separation of the Moon from the earth.

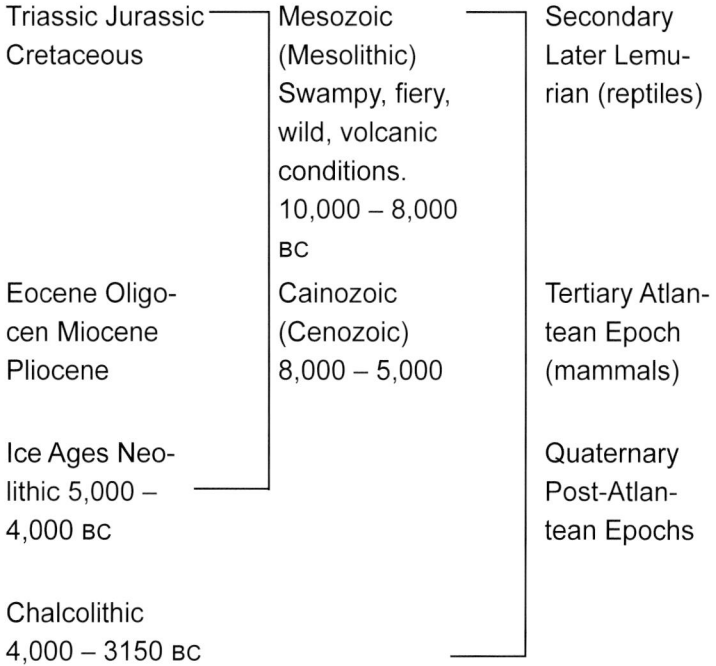

Triassic Jurassic Cretaceous	Mesozoic (Mesolithic) Swampy, fiery, wild, volcanic conditions. 10,000 – 8,000 BC	Secondary Later Lemurian (reptiles)
Eocene Oligocen Miocene Pliocene	Cainozoic (Cenozoic) 8,000 – 5,000	Tertiary Atlantean Epoch (mammals)
Ice Ages Neolithic 5,000 – 4,000 BC		Quaternary Post-Atlantean Epochs
Chalcolithic 4,000 – 3150 BC		

Reference: 'Epochs of Evolution' by John Waterman, Publ. in *The Golden Blade* 1957

TIME CHART by W. Scott-Elliot

Rock Strata.	Depth of Strata. Feet.	Races of Men.	Cataclysms.	Animals.	Plants.
Laurentian / Cambrian / silurian } Archilithic or Primordial	70,000	First Root Race which being Astral could leave no fossil remains.		Skull-less Animals.	Forests of gigantic Tangles and other Thallus Plants.
Devonian / coal / Permian } Palæolithic or Primary.	42,000	Second Root Race which was Etheric.		Fish.	Fern Forests.
Triassic / Jurassic / Cretaceous } Mesolithic or Secondary	15,000	Third Root Race or Lemurian.	Lemuria is said to have perished before the beginning of the Eocene age.	Reptiles.	Pine and Palm Forests.
Eocene / Miocene / Pliocene } Cenolithic or Tertiary.	5,000	Fourth Root Race or Atlantean.	The main continent of Atlantis was destroyed in the Miocene period about 800,000 years ago. Second great catastrophe ? about 200,000 years ago.	Mammals.	Forests of Deciduous Trees.
Diluvial or Pleistocene / Alluvial } Quaternary or Anthropolithic	500	Fifth Root Race or Aryan.	Third great catastrophe about 80,000 years ago. Final submergence of Poseidonis 9564 BC	More differentiated Mammals.	Cultivated Forests.

BIBLIOGRAPHY

Rudolf Steiner:

At Home in the Universe (CW 231), SteinerBooks 2000

The Being of Man and his Future Evolution (CW 107), Rudolf Steiner Press, 1981. Republished as *Disease, Karma and Healing*, Rudolf Steiner Press 2013

Cosmic Memory, Atlantis and Lemuria (CW 11), SteinerBooks 1987

Egyptian Myths and Mysteries (CW 106), SteinerBooks 1971

Festivals and Their Meaning, Rudolf Steiner Press 2002

Foundations of Esotericism (CW 93a), Rudolf Steiner Press 2019

From Crystals to Crocodiles, Answers to Questions (CW 347), Rudolf Steiner Press 2002

Genesis, Secrets of the Bible Story of Creation (CW 122), Rudolf Steiner Press 2002

The Influence of Spiritual Beings upon Man (CW 102), Anthroposophic Press, 1961. Republished as *Good and Evil Spirits*, Rudolf Steiner Press 2014

Life Beyond Death, Rudolf Steiner Press 2003

The Lord's Prayer, Rudolf Steiner Press 2006

Mystery Knowledge and Mystery Centres (CW 232), Rudolf Steiner Press, 1998

Occult Science (CW 13), Rudolf Steiner Press, 2013

Sexuality, Love and Partnership, Compiled and Edited by Margaret Jonas, Rudolf Steiner Press 2013

The Spiritual Guidance of the Individual and Humanity (CW 15), Anthroposophic Press 1991

Theosophy of the Rosicrucian (CW 99), Rudolf Steiner Press 1966. Republished as *Rosicrucian Wisdom*, Rudolf Steiner Press 2000

Universe, Earth, Human Being (CW 105), Rudolf Steiner Press 2022

('CW' refers to the Collected Works catalogue number.)

Other Authors:

The Archetypal Human-Animal, Angela Lord, Temple Lodge Publishing 2022

The Care and Development of the Senses, Willi Aeppli, Steiner Schools Fellowship 1993

Genesis, Creation and the Patriarchs, Emil Bock, Floris Books 1983

The Language of Colour in the First Goetheanum, A Study of Rudolf Steiner's Art, Hilde Raske, Rudolf Steiner Press 2023

The Living Origin of Rocks and Minerals, Walter Cloos, Floris Books 2015

Man and Animal, Hermann Poppelbaum, Rudolf Steiner Press 2014

'Searching for Lemuria', Maarten Ekama, *New View* magazine, Summer 2017

The Secret Doctrine, H. P. Blavatsky, 1888

The Story of Atlantis and the Lost Lemuria, William Scott-Elliot, 1925

A note from the publisher

For more than a quarter of a century, **Temple Lodge Publishing** has made available new thought, ideas and research in the field of spiritual science.

Anthroposophy, as founded by Rudolf Steiner (1861-1925), is commonly known today through its practical applications, principally in education (Steiner-Waldorf schools) and agriculture (biodynamic food and wine). But behind this outer activity stands the core discipline of spiritual science, which continues to be developed and updated. True science can never be static and anthroposophy is living knowledge.

Our list features some of the best contemporary spiritual-scientific work available today, as well as introductory titles. So, visit us online at **www.templelodge.com** and join our emailing list for news on new titles.

If you feel like supporting our work, you can do so by buying our books or making a direct donation (we are a non-profit/charitable organisation).

office@templelodge.com

☀ TEMPLE LODGE

For the finest books of Science and Spirit